Contents

My place

MY PLACE

My Mum
My mum is a teacher; her hobbies are reading and baking.

My Dad
My dad's hobbies are birdwatching and playing badminton.

At home

My Grandparents
I have two grandmas and one grandpa.

Pets
I have a dog called Suzy; my Grandma looks after her.

My brothers
I have two step-brothers who have just left school. One is called Marky and the other is called Julian.

My friends
Steven Wood
Alan Breckon
Duncan Crabbe

My teachers
Mr Green
Mr Wood
Mr Brown

At school

People I know
nearly everybody in the school except for the fourth and fifth years.

My enemies

My friend
Steven Wood

Where I live

People I know
Nearly everybody in our road.

My parents' friends
The Wilsons
The Sayles

What to do

These are Gareth's and Jill's maps of their place. They've drawn three diagrams of their place:

    at home
    at school
    where they live.

You are going to make a map of 'your place'.

1. Begin with **home**. Copy the pattern Jill and Gareth have used and write about the people at **your home**.
2. Now do the same for **school**.
3. Now for **where you live**.

Oxford Secondary English

Dimensions

Book 2

John Seely
Frank Green
Graham Nutbrown

Oxford University Press 1988

Oxford University Press, Walton Street, Oxford OX2 6DP

Oxford New York Toronto
Delhi Bombay Calcutta Madras Karachi
Petaling Jaya Singapore Hong Kong Tokyo
Nairobi Dar es Salaam Cape Town
Melbourne Auckland

and associated companies in
Beirut Berlin Ibadan Nicosia

Oxford is a trade mark of Oxford University Press

ISBN 0 19 833169 X

Phototypeset by Graphicraft Typesetters Ltd., Hong Kong
Printed in Hong Kong

MY PLACE

My teaches
Mr Ryan is my French teacher. he also used to teach my brothers Ian and Martin.

AT SCHOOL

My Friends
Emma lives near to me; we walk up to school together.

My Mum
My mum does not go to work. She's the chairman of Trefoil, and Action for the crippled child.

AT HOME

My Brothers
Ian, my older brother, is a Quantity Surveyor in Winchester. Martin is working at Dales as an Electrical Engineer.

My Dad
My dad works as an electrical contractor. He is also the Honorary Secretary of the lifeboat.

My Neighbours
My neighbour is Mr Roy Mason. He was the Minister for Northern Ireland.

WHERE I LIVE

Talking points

1 Which of your three patterns has the most information on it?
2 Why is this?
3 Which of them is the most important to you?
4 Why?
5 Could you draw other diagrams that would describe 'your place'? If so, what would they show?

Whose place?

Making a table

1 Draw three columns.
2 In the first column, make a list of all the different jobs that are being done in this house.
3 In the second column, write down who is doing each job.
4 In the third column, write down who does that job in your home.

Questions

In many homes particular household jobs are done by particular people. Some jobs are done by mum, and dad never offers to help her. In the same way mum never does dad's jobs. Think about these questions:

1 Is this a good idea?
2 Is there anything about certain household jobs that means a particular person should always do them?
3 What are your reasons for saying that?

Writing

Write down your opinion of this idea: 'All household jobs should be shared equally by all people in the family. Sex and age don't make any difference at all.'

I'm the youngest in our house

I'm the youngest in our house so it goes like this:

My brother comes in and says:
'Tell him to clear the fluff
out from under his bed.'
Mum says,
'Clear the fluff
out from under your bed.'
Father says,
'You heard what your mother said.'
'What?' I say.
'The fluff,' he says.
'Clear the fluff
out from under your bed.'
So I say,
'There's fluff under his bed, too,
you know.'
So father says,
'But we're talking about the fluff
under *your* bed.'
'You will clear it up
won't you?' Mum says.
So now my brother – all puffed up –
says,
'Clear the fluff
out from under your bed,
clear the fluff
out from under your bed.'
Now I'm angry. I am angry.
So I say – what shall I say?
I say,
'Shuttup Stinks
YOU CAN'T RULE MY LIFE.'

Michael Rosen

Questions

Michael Rosen's poem gives the point of view of one person in a family.

1 Who is that person?
2 What do you think it would be like to have him in your family?
3 What is his point of view?
4 Do you sympathise with him? What are your reasons?
5 Is your family like this?

Writing: points of view

Everybody in a family has a point of view. Sometimes they don't agree. Sometimes this leads to conversations like the one in the poem.

Preparation

Write short answers to these questions.

What do you get angry about at home?

Think of a conversation you might have: Who would be talking? How would it go? How would it start and end?

Writing

Now write your conversation. Here are some titles you could use:

> I'm the busiest in our house
> I'm the oldest in our house
> In our house no one except me ever . . .
> Why does nobody except me
>   ever clear/clean/tidy the . . . .
> I'm fed up with this
>   family. Everybody always . . . .

Does it make sense?

Peter Dereham lived in a top floor flat. All the buildings in Frenchay Place are flats. So he must have lived in Frenchay Place. His best friend Darren was a roller-skating enthusiast. I was rather surprised because I wouldn't have thought Peter was likely to be interested in roller-skating.

This piece of writing contains two statements that do not make sense. They do not follow on from what has been said before.

1   Can you work out what they are?
2   Can you explain why they don't follow on?

Now you try

Each of these arguments makes sense if you complete the middle sentence properly. For each one write out the correct middle sentence.

1   Chips are my favourite food.
I am eating . . . .
Therefore I am eating chips.

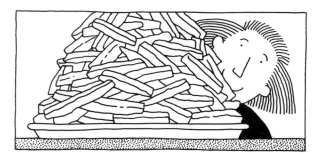

2   I enjoy watching TV.
I am . . . .
Therefore I am enjoying what I am doing.

3   John is taller than Bill.
Bill . . . .
Therefore John is taller than Mary.

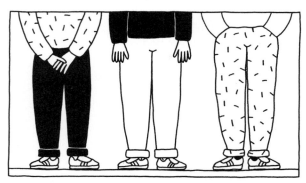

4   James copies from Wayne.
. . . .
Therefore James gets everything right.

True or false?

The next arguments are in pairs. One makes sense and one doesn't. Which is which?

5a   I like all records by Ferretman.
This record is by Ferretman.
Therefore I like this record.

5b   I like all records by Ferretman.
I like this record.
Therefore this record is by Ferretman.

6a Bracelets over 150 years old are valuable.
This bracelet is valuable.
Therefore this bracelet is over 150 years old.

6b Bracelets over 150 years old are valuable.
This bracelet is over 150 years old.
Therefore this bracelet is valuable.

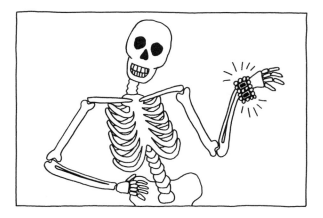

Logical or true?

When this kind of argument is used properly, we say that it is **logical**. This means that it makes sense. That isn't the same thing as saying it is **true**. It is only true if the first two sentences are true. Compare these two arguments:

a) All the teachers in our school are employed by the County Council.
Mrs Painswick teaches at our school.
Therefore Mrs Painswick is employed by the County Council.

b) All the teachers in our school live to be 150.
Mrs Painswick teaches at our school.
Therefore Mrs Painswick will live to be 150.

Argument a) is logical and true.
Argument b) is logical but it isn't true, because the first sentence is not true.

You try

Divide these arguments into two groups:

logical and true
logical but untrue.

7 Carpet tiles are good to eat.
Easifloor Ltd. makes carpet tiles.
Therefore Easifloor Ltd. is a food manufacturer.

8 You must be able to swim to play water polo.
Peter can't swim a stroke.
Therefore Peter can't play water polo.

9 This book is made of paper.
Paper will not burn.
Therefore this book will not burn.

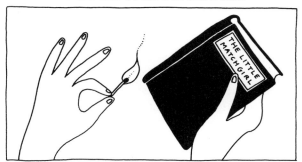

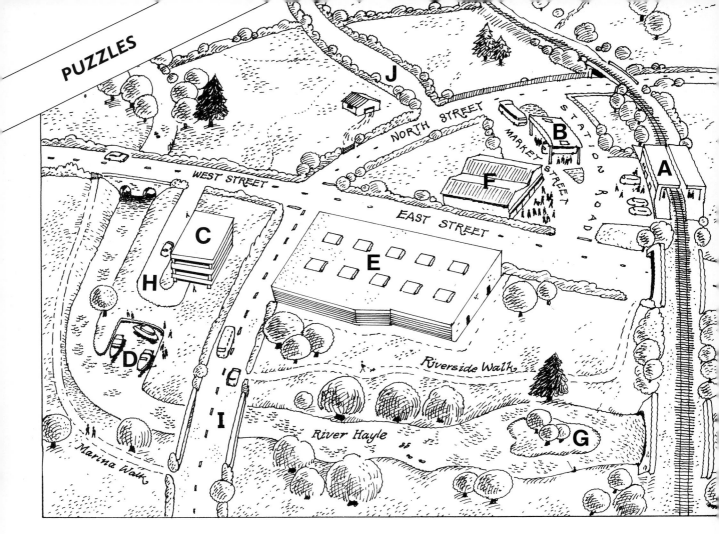

A tour of Helton

On this map of Helton, some of the names have been removed and replaced by letters. Study the map and read the description of the town walk. Then work out where the missing names should go, and find the answers to the questions.

Town walk

Come out of the multi-storey car-park and turn right into Quay Street. Go along to the end, where it meets West Street. Turn right and go as far as the crossroads. On your left is North Street, and straight ahead is East Street.

Don't take either of these, but turn right along South Street. Just before you reach the River Hayle, turn left along the river bank. Follow Riverside Walk past the island called Little Eyot. Turn left alongside the railway line, until you come to East Street. Turn left and then right into Station Road. On your right is the railway station and on your left is the covered market. Continue along Station Road, passing the bus station on your left. When you come to North Street turn left and walk past the end of Merton Road (on your right). Keep going until you reach the crossroads.

Missing names:

Bus station
Quay Street
Covered market
Multi-storey car-park
Shopping centre

Hayle marina
Railway station
Little Eyot
South Street
Merton Road

Questions

1　Where are you at the end of the tour?
2　What is the quickest way back to the multi-storey car-park?
3　Is there any other way you could get there?
4　Which of the missing names is not mentioned in the town walk?
5　Where are they on the map?

Anagrams

Each of these is an anagram of a well-known British city:

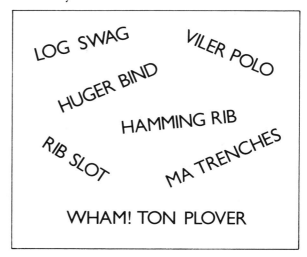

LOG SWAG

VILER POLO

HUGER BIND

HAMMING RIB

RIB SLOT

MA TRENCHES

WHAM! TON PLOVER

Work out which cities they are.

Coded buildings

This puzzle uses an **alphabet slip** code.

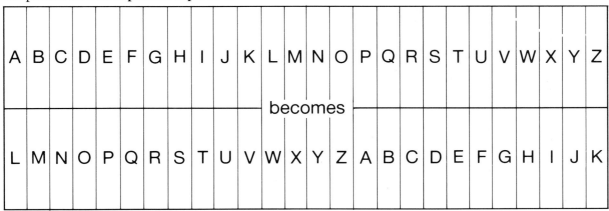

A	B	C	D	E	F	G	H	I	J	K	L	M	N	O	P	Q	R	S	T	U	V	W	X	Y	Z

becomes

L	M	N	O	P	Q	R	S	T	U	V	W	X	Y	Z	A	B	C	D	E	F	G	H	I	J	K

So CAGE becomes NLRP.

Decode this list of buildings:

NLDEWP　　　　NZEELRP
MFYRLWZH　　　NLESPOCLW
ALWLNP　　　　QLNEZCJ

Memories of home

A Jamaica to me represents all that is fabulous. I can remember on our way home from school we would stop to pick oranges or tangerines or guavas or any fruit that happened to be in season. The best climbers would climb up trees and pick the fruit. The others kept a look-out, because of course the fruit did not belong to us or even to our families; then joy of joys would be when the farmer was sighted coming along. Of course no one wanted to be caught. Heavens! If that happened you would get such a hiding.

Vashti Ledford *So This is England*

B We lived in a tall, yellow brick house in Manchester, half-way between Withington and Fallowfield. From the nursery windows you could watch the trams rattle by across the cobbles. Number 10 Wilmslow Road was an ugly house, four storeys high. The rooms were large and draughty; gas lighting left the lofty ceilings in shadow. Coal for the open fires was carried up in scuttles from the cellar. The only bathroom was a cramped cubby-hole under the roof, with a very nasty, narrow bath, a gurgling cistern, and no light all day long, except for one feeble gas jet.

C.A. Lejeune *Thank You For Having Me*

C When I think of our winters at the Bu they turn into one long winter evening round the stove playing draughts or listening to the fiddle or the melodeon, or sitting still while my father told of his witches or fairicks. The winter gathered us into one room as it gathered the cattle into the stable and the byre; the sky came closer; the lamps were lit at three or four in the afternoon, and then the great evening lay before us like a world: an evening filled with talk, stories, games, music, and lamplight.

Edwin Muir *An Autobiography*

Questions

1. Which of the three places sounds the most interesting and attractive? Why?
2. Which sounds least interesting and attractive? Why?

Passage A

3. When did the children pick fruit?
4. What happened if they were caught?
5. The author says Jamaica was 'fabulous'. Why does he think so?

Passage B

6. How high was the house?
7. How was it heated?
8. Would you have liked to live in it? What are your reasons?

Passage C

9. Make a list of the things they did on the long winter evenings.
10. At about what time did it get dark?
11. How do their winter evenings compare with yours?

Words

In this table column 1 contains words from A, B, and C. Column 2 contains their meanings **in the wrong order**. Copy out the table, putting the meanings in the right order.

	Column 1: Words	Column 2: Meanings
A	fabulous	fairies
	guavas	wonderful
B	cistern	tropical fruits
C	melodeon	place for cattle
	byre	water tank
	fairicks	musical instrument

Writing

The writers of these descriptions were all describing the place where they lived as children. They are writing about their **memories** of childhood. They remember **facts** and **feelings**.

Preparation

1. Think about the place where you live now. When you are old, what will you remember about it?
2. Make a list of the **feelings** you will remember about it.
3. Make a list of the **facts** you will remember about it.

Writing

Imagine that you are an old person remembering your childhood home. Write a description of **The place where I grew up.**

13

Where did it happen?

In a story the **setting** is where the action takes
place. The story may tell you quite a lot about
the setting: not only where it is, but also what
it looks like, and what is going on there.

Nobody was at the airport to meet him.

One of the stewardesses had told him there was a place called
the rendezvous area where you could go and wait if your friends
hadn't turned up when the plane landed. So that was where he
went. It was next to the information desk, a set of plush-covered
benches, striped in pink and brown, with a few anxious people
sitting on them, gazing about in every direction. But Cosmo
preferred to stand, leaning against the trolley that held his luggage
– two cases, a carry-on bag, and a tennis-racket. He stared at the
mass of people, streaming up and down the airport concourse,
wondering how he would ever know which one was looking for
him.

Joan Aiken   *The Shadow Guests*

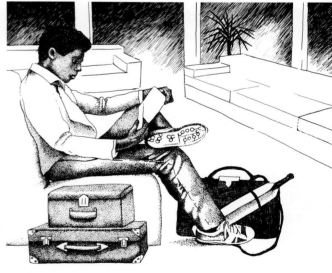

Questions

Which of these pictures gives the best idea of
the setting? How many mistakes can you spot
in the other one?

The waiting-room

Here is the start of a story set in a waiting-room. It might be any kind of waiting-room — a doctor's or dentist's, for example. Some parts of the description have been missed out.

1 Decide what kind of waiting-room you want it to be.
2 Think how the spaces might be filled. There aren't any *right* answers — just make the place as interesting as possible.
3 Copy it out and fill in the missing bits.

Lucy opened the door of the waiting-room and walked in. She looked round. In the middle of the room was a _____ table and on it there were _____. The room was silent except for _____ of the _____ in the corner. Above the fireplace there was a _____ and on the mantlepiece were some _____. The room was _____ because outside it was _____. Lucy felt _____ and _____. She turned on the light and as she did so she saw a _____ lying on the carpet. 'That's odd,' she thought and picked it up. She sat down in a _____ chair to look at it carefully. Then she heard _____ coming from the next room. She wondered what was happening in there. She began to wish she hadn't come.

Writing

Continue this story about the waiting-room. Include the things you have mentioned. What did she pick up off the floor? What were on the mantlepiece? Why were they important?

Sometimes the description of a place can tell us more than what the place **looks** like. What feelings do you get about this place?

I landed with a thump, the breath going out of my chest, and lay still, my face stuck into wet, soft earth. Everything was black around. There wasn't a sound. The darkness in this hole was thicker than ever and the smell was even grottier.

My hand struck wood-planks standing up. I ran my finger along it. That was funny. It was a table, a trestle-table, like dad had in our basement to do his do-it-yourself on. I felt better right away. A table can't do you any harm. There might be chairs as well — I thought — and a sideboard, and cupboards and a cooker . . . My hands slid along the top and knocked on something. There was a tinny sound. My fingers touched metal, small and round — a mug and a basin next to it. My fingers slipped inside the basin and jerked back of their own accord. The inside was all soft and mushy, like cloth or leather gone rotten. It was weird.

My knee knocked hard on more wood — a three-legged stool. Sitting down I began to run my hands along the table-top again. A bottle. The smell from it was like nothing on earth — whisky or beer gone bad. Somebody had made himself comfortable here. But I wasn't. I had to get out.

Robert Leeson *Challenge in the Dark*

The caravan

The caravan was our house and our home. It was a real old gypsy wagon with big wheels and fine patterns painted all over it in yellow and red and blue. My father said it was at least a hundred and fifty years old. Many gypsy children, he said, had been born in it and had grown up within its wooden walls. With a horse to pull it, the old caravan must have wandered for thousands of miles along the roads and lanes of England. But now its wanderings were over, and because the wooden spokes in the wheels were beginning to rot, my father had propped it up underneath with bricks.

There was only one room in the caravan and it wasn't much bigger than a fair-sized modern bathroom. It was a narrow room, the shape of the caravan itself, and against the back wall were two bunk beds, one above the other. The top one was my father's, the bottom one mine.

Although we had electric lights in the workshop, we were not allowed to have them in the caravan. The electricity people said it was unsafe to put wires into something as old and rickety as that. So we got our heat and light in much the same way as the gypsies had done years ago. There was a wood-burning stove with a chimney that went up through the roof, and this kept us warm in winter. There was a paraffin burner on which to boil a kettle or cook a stew, and there was a paraffin lamp hanging from the ceiling.

When I needed a bath, my father would heat a kettle of water and pour it into a basin. Then he would strip me naked and scrub me all over, standing up. This, I think, got me just as clean as if I were washed in a bath – probably cleaner because I didn't finish up sitting in my own dirty water.

For furniture, we had two chairs and a small table, and those, apart from a tiny chest of drawers, were all the home comforts we possessed. They were all we needed.

The lavatory was a funny little wooden hut standing in the field some way from the caravan. It was fine in summertime, but I can tell you that sitting out there on a snowy day in winter was like sitting in a fridge.

Immediately behind the caravan was an old apple tree. It bore lovely apples that ripened in the middle of September and you could go on picking them for the next four or five weeks. Some of the boughs of the tree hung right over the caravan and when the wind blew the apples down in the night they often landed on our roof. I would hear them going **thump** . . . **thump thump** . . . above my head as I lay in my bunk, but those noises never frightened me because I knew exactly what was making them.

I really loved living in the gypsy caravan. I loved it especially in the evenings when I was tucked up in my bunk and my father was telling me stories. The paraffin lamp was turned low, and I could see lumps of wood glowing red-hot in the old stove and wonderful it was to be lying there snug and warm in my bunk in that little room. Most wonderful of all was the feeling that when I went to sleep, my father would still be there, very close to me, sitting in his chair by the fire, or lying in the bunk above my own.

Roald Dahl   *Danny the Champion of the World*

Understanding the story

1   Make a list of all the things there were in the caravan.
2   Work out where all these things were.
3   Draw a picture or plan to show where everything was inside the caravan.
4   Explain how Danny and his father:
     a) kept clean   b) kept warm.
5   Danny 'loved living in that gypsy caravan.' What reasons does he give to explain this?

Thinking about the story

1   Would you like to live in a caravan like this? What are your reasons?
2   Here are two lists of words. They are in pairs. Choose one word from each pair to describe your impression of the caravan and what it would be like to live in it.

     quaint   old fashioned
     snug   stuffy
     unusual   inconvenient
     neat   cramped

3   Use the words you have chosen in one or more sentences to describe your thoughts about life in the caravan.

Writing about home

Preparation

What does the word **home** mean to you?
     The building you live in?
     The furniture?
     The people?
     Or what?
Think about this and make a list of the most important things **home** means.

Writing

Now write your thoughts and feelings about **Home**.

A room of my own

Have you ever dreamed about designing your own room, or even your own house? In this Special you can do just that. On this page there are drawings that show one person's ideas about how parts of the room might look. On the opposite page are instructions and advice on how to go about designing your room.

What to do

1 Look at the pictures and think about **your** ideas for your own room.
2 Make a list of the main things you want, with a brief description of each one. There is a **checklist** on this page to help you.
3 Think about how you want the room arranged.
4 Copy the plan outline on this page. It is to a scale of 1 : 50. If you keep your plan to the same scale, then you will know that each centimetre on the plan is equal to 50 centimetres in the room. (Or one inch equals four feet.)
5 Draw on your plan the positions of the furniture. You can use the shapes on this page as a guide; they are to the same scale as the room outline.
6 Round the outside of your plan, put any labels or explanations that are needed. (For example, you might want to write notes about the colour the walls will be.)
7 Finish off by writing a description of **A room of my own.** Describe the furniture and the appearance of your room, and explain **why** you have decided to arrange things in the way you have.

Checklist

Your room should contain:
   somewhere to sleep,
   somewhere to sit down,
   somewhere to store clothing,
   somewhere to do homework.
It could also include:
   somewhere to keep books,
   somewhere to store records,
   somewhere to display posters and pictures
      and other things,
   a hi-fi.

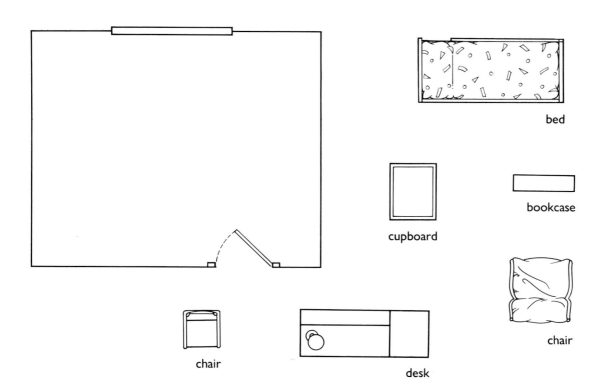

bed

bookcase

cupboard

chair

chair

desk

Dream house

This is where you can really let yourself go – designing your dream house. Look at the pictures on these two pages and then follow these instructions.

What to do

1 Look at the pictures on page 20. Think about what kind of house your dream house would be. Would it be like any of these? Or something completely different?

2 Write a description of your dream house from the outside. Include these points:
   Where it is.
   What kind of building it is.
   What the garden is like.

3 Draw a sketch of what it looks like.

4 Look at these pictures. Think about what your dream house would be like inside.

5 Make a list of the main rooms.

6 Make a list of the most important things about each room: furniture, decoration, and so on.

7 Now imagine what it would be like to live in your dream house. Think about how you would use the various rooms. Now write a description of **A day in my dream house**.

Friendship

You're never alone with Friend

Lennie is a loner. He lives with his mother in a motel. During the holidays he sometimes visits a deserted house near his home on the other side of a small lake.

In the centre of the lake he suddenly wished he were back at the motel again. He tried to lose himself in his thoughts.

What if the Partridge family's bus had broken down and they were stranded and while he was rowing across the lake he started singing and they heard him and asked him to join the group and gave him his own electric guitar? While he was imagining himself in a white fringed suit on the stage with the Partridges, he lost interest.

He shifted thoughts.

What if he were the last person on earth? He had seen that the week before on *Thursday Night Movie*. A plague had come and disintegrated everyone but one person. Now Lennie imagined himself that person, rowing across the lake wondering what had happened to everyone else.

He rowed more slowly. His oars dragged in the water. He felt as lonely as if he really were the last person on earth.

To change his mood he imagined a commercial.

'To help that lonely feeling,' the announcer would say, 'buy Friend, the doll that's as big and as real as you are.'

He brightened. He imagined the announcer's voice saying, 'Yes, with Friend, you'll always have someone to talk to.' There would be a shot of him and Friend talking and laughing on a park bench.

'With Friend you'll never have to go to the movies alone.'

There would be a shot of him and Friend entering a movie theatre. The announcer would say quietly, 'And remember, Friend comes with a special I.D. card that lets him enter all movie theatres and sports events for half price.'

Lennie smiled. He began to row again. He felt better. He imagined the end of the commercial with him and Friend strolling along a country road. The announcer would say, 'Yes, take Friend everywhere you go and –' then a choir of a hundred voices would sing – '**You'll never be alone.**'

Lennie was close to the shore now, and he eased up on his rowing. He drifted the rest of the way. When his boat touched shore, Lennie got out quickly. He pulled his boat up under the long waving branches of the willow tree. He started for the house.

Lennie was on the front porch of the stone house now. He peered through the window.

In his mind the announcer reminded him, 'Whenever you enter an empty house, take Friend along. Yes, remember, no house is ever empty with Friend.'

He imagined Friend peering through the window too, glancing at Lennie, waiting.

'Let's go in,' Lennie would say. Friend would nod in agreement. 'Follow me.' Another nod and Friend would fall in behind.

Betsy Byars   *The TV Kid*

Questions

1   What kind of person do you think Lennie is?
2   What makes you think this?
3   What does Lennie think are the most important things about friendship?
4   How do you know this?
5   What do you think are the most important things about friendship?
6   This is a list of things that different people think are important in a friendship. Write them out with the most important at the top and the least important at the bottom.
A friend should:
a)   Be loyal.
b)   Always tell you the truth.
c)   Be reliable.
d)   Go along with what you want.
e)   Always tell you when there is something wrong.
f)   Like the same things that you do.
g)   Stick up for you, even when you are in the wrong.
h)   Always trust you.

Writing

1   Lennie has invented a TV advert for a product concerned with friendship. He has thought up:
the product,
a name for it,
how it will be advertised on TV.
You do the same. Either invent your own product, or choose one of these:
a)   An aerosol that you spray on yourself so that everyone wants to be your friend.
b)   A pair of glasses that you can wear when you want to read people's minds, to find out whether they feel friendly towards you.
Now choose a name for the product, and then describe how you would advertise it on TV.

23

People

What they look like

When you are describing a person, there's not much point in just saying, 'She had two legs, two arms and a head'. You need to pick out some ways in which the person is different from other people.

Writing about a picture

Look at the three people on the facing page. For each one:

1   Study the picture carefully.
2   Decide on the most important things about that person. It might be:
    - shape of head
    - age
    - clothes
    - shape of mouth
    - height
    - shape of eyes
    - hands
    - physique (body)
    - colour of hair, eyes, etc.
3   Now write a description, including these points and adding anything else you think is important about that person.

Writing about a friend

Now try writing this kind of description about a person you know well. See if you can describe him or her so that other people will recognise who it is.

Their personalities

Describing what someone looks like does not always tell us much about what sort of person he or she is. We need to add some information about their **personality**. There are lots of different kinds of personality. What different kinds can you think of? Here are some words to help you:

happy	serious	bossy
depressed	bad-tempered	kind
strict	wicked	jolly
adventurous	proud	carefree
fearless	nervous	lazy

Which of these words do you think might fit the three people in the pictures on the facing page?

Making a character chart

Copy out this chart. Put each of the words in the list into one of the three columns. Now add at least six more words that you have thought of yourself.

Good points	Neutral points	Bad points
happy	serious	lazy

Writing

Write two short character descriptions of people you know, or people you have made up:

1   using words from the 'bad' list,
2   using words from the 'good' list.

My father

My father without the slightest doubt, was the most marvellous and exciting father any boy ever had.

You might think, if you didn't know him well, that he was a stern and serious man. He wasn't. He was actually a wildly funny person. What made him appear serious was the fact that he never smiled with his mouth. He did it all with his eyes. He had brilliant blue eyes and when he thought of something funny, his eyes would flash and if you looked carefully, you could actually see a tiny little golden spark dancing in the middle of each eye. But the mouth never moved.

I was glad my father was an eye-smiler. It meant he never gave me a fake smile because it's impossible to make your eyes twinkle if you aren't feeling twinkly yourself. A mouth-smile is different. You can fake a mouth-smile any time you want, simply by moving your lips. I've also learned that a real mouth-smile always has an eye-smile to go with it, so watch out, I say, when someone smiles at you with his mouth but the eyes stay the same. It's sure to be bogus.

My father was not what you would call an educated man and I doubt if he had read twenty books in his life. But he was a marvellous storyteller. He used to make up a bedtime story for me every single night, and the best ones were turned into serials and went on for many nights running. One of them, which must have gone on for at least fifty nights, was about an enormous fellow called the Big Friendly Giant, or the BFG for short. The BFG was three times as tall as an ordinary man and his hands were as big as wheelbarrows...

Occasionally, as he told his stories, my father would stride up and down waving his arms and waggling his fingers. But mostly he would sit close to me on the edge of my bunk and speak very softly.

Roald Dahl   *Danny the Champion of the World*

Question

Which of the pictures above do you think looks most like Danny's father? Why?

Writing

Now write a full character description of:

1   Someone you know.
2   One of the people in the pictures, but not Danny's father.

25

Characters

Here are some more pictures of people.

Writing about a character

1 Choose one of the people in the pictures.
2 Give him or her a name.
3 Think about this person's life. Here are some questions to help you:

How old is s/he?
What kind of job has s/he got?
What kind of house does s/he live in?
Does s/he live in the town or in the country?

What pets has s/he got?
What kind of car does s/he drive?
What kind of voice or accent has s/he got?
What nasty habits has s/he got?
What is s/he good at?
Is s/he married?
Has s/he got any children?
What was s/he like at school?

Can you think of any more questions yourself?
4 Make a list of all the things you have decided about your character.

Turning it into a story

An ordinary day in someone's life isn't usually a particularly interesting story, but it's a good starting-point.

Now think of something interesting, unusual, or exciting which happens to change the day. Here are some ideas:

Receiving important news which changes the character's life.

An accident.

Meeting a person who is strange, frightening, unexpected.

Write down your idea and think about how your character will behave and what s/he will do. Make some notes.

> Mary is cycling to the charity shop. There is an accident just in front of her. An old lady is knocked down.
>
> She is very upset, but she goes to help. She knows a bit of first aid and no one else there knows what to do, so she takes charge.
>
> The old lady is taken to hospital. When she recovers, she asks to speak to Mary.

A day in the life

Now imagine that you are the person you have invented. Think about an ordinary day in **your** life.

An account of your day

Write down a timetable of that day. Now use your timetable to write an account of that day.

> Tuesday is my day for helping at the Charity shop. I got up as usual at seven o'clock and got breakfast for Jane and Emma. They didn't want any breakfast again, but I made them have some cornflakes. Emma made a fuss!

Writing the story

Now tell the story. This time don't write it as if you are the person. Write it **about** the character.

> It was just another Tuesday as Mary Hughes set out for the charity shop. She had given Jane and Emma their breakfast and taken them to school. As she got on her bike she noticed that it was just beginning to rain.
>
> The road was quite slippery....

ACTIVITIES

What went wrong?

On these two pages are a poem and a picture story. Each is about a friendship that went wrong. For each one, this is what you do:

1 Tell the story of what happened.
2 Explain why you think the friendship went wrong.
3 Say what special qualities of friendship are talked about in the story.

I thought a lot of you

I thought you were my friend,
  I thought you said you'd help;
I thought I could trust you,
  I thought I could count on you;
I thought you were loyal,
  I thought you would understand;
I thought I made it sound straightforward,
  I thought I had someone to talk to;
I thought you had an answer,
  I thought you were a good listener;
I thought I was telling in confidence,
  I thought I wasn't being stupid;
I thought you wouldn't make a fool of me,
  I thought you weren't going to tell a soul;
    I thought wrong!

P.S. Blackman (Jnr)

Words taken from Gospel according to Matthew, Chapter 27.

28

Before the cock crows

GIRL: Weren't you too with Jesus, the man from Galilee?
PETER: I don't know what you're talking about.

JESUS: Tonight every one of you will lose his faith in me.
PETER: Even if everyone should lose his faith in you, I never will!
JESUS: I tell you, Peter, that tonight before the cock crows, you will disown me three times.
PETER: Even if it means dying with you, I will never disown you.

GIRL: This man was with Jesus of
       Nazareth.
PETER: I don't know the man!

MAN: You certainly are one of them.
      It's obvious from your accent.
PETER: I tell you I don't know the man!

Friendly poems
Billy Dreamer's fantastic friends

The Incredible Hulk came to tea,
Robin was with him too,
Batman stayed at home that night
Because his bat had flu.

Superman called to say hello
And Spiderman spun us a joke.
Dynamite Sue was supposed to come
But she went up in smoke.

The Invisible Man might have called.
But as I wasn't sure,
I left an empty chair and bun
Beside the kitchen door.

They signed my autograph book,
But I dropped it in the fire.
Now whenever I tell my friends
They say I'm a terrible liar.

But incredible people *do* call round
('Specially when I'm alone).
And if they don't, and I get bored,
I call them on the phone.

Brian Patten

Writing

Write a poem or a story about one of these
subjects:
    My own fantastic friends
    Dave Dirt goes on holiday
    Dave Dirt's fantastic friends
    The day Dave Dirt came to tea
    with my family

Dave Dirt came to dinner

Dave Dirt came to dinner
    And he stuck his chewing-gum
Underneath the table
    And it didn't please my Mum

And it didn't please my Granny
    Who was quite a sight to see
When she got up from the table
    With the gum stuck to her knee

Where she put her cup and saucer
    When she sat and drank her tea
And the saucer and the chewing-gum
    Got stuck as stuck can be

And she staggered round the kitchen
    With a saucer on her skirt –
No, it didn't please my Granny
    But it
        PLEASED
        DAVE
        DIRT

Kit Wright

Going out with the gang

Anna likes roller-skating and football, but she can't go out on Wednesdays, Fridays or Sundays.

Brian's a music freak and loves BMXing, but he's never free on a Tuesday or a Thursday.

Charlotte only likes going to the pictures or listening to music. She can go out any day except Tuesday and Saturday.

Dave is keen on roller-skating and BMXing. He says any day is fine as long as it's not a Monday or a Wednesday.

Eddie likes going to the pictures and always enjoys football, so long as it's not on a Friday or a Tuesday.

Fiona's favourite activities are music and football. She is free any time, except Sundays and Mondays.

There are six of us in our gang.

The trouble is that we can never sort out where we are going or when to go.

True or false?

Some of these statements are true and some are false. Which is which?

1 Anna and Dave like going roller-skating on a Tuesday.
2 Eddie and Fiona like going to football on a Tuesday.
3 Brian and Dave enjoy BMXing on a Sunday.
4 Charlotte and Eddie sometimes go to the pictures on a Wednesday.

What can we do?

Use the information provided to work out the answers to these questions:

1 Anna would like to go out with Eddie. When can they go out together, and where should they go?
2 Brian and Charlotte would like to go to a pop concert together. When can they go? Would Fiona like to go with them? If all three went together, what day would it be?
3 Dave and Eddie are both free on three days. Which are they?
4 There are three people who like football. Who are they? When can all three go to a football match together?
5 On what days are most members of the gang free?

31

The Pupil's Friend

Explaining

1 Study the drawing and work out what this machine does.
2 Write a clear explanation of how the machine works.
3 How would you improve **The Pupil's Friend?** Make a list of things it ought to be able to do.

Making up an advertisement

You are going to write an advertisement for **The Pupil's Friend** to appear in a comic or magazine.

1 Think of the most important things you want to say about the machine.
2 Think about what the page should look like.
3 Now design and draw your advertisement.

How a water-pistol works

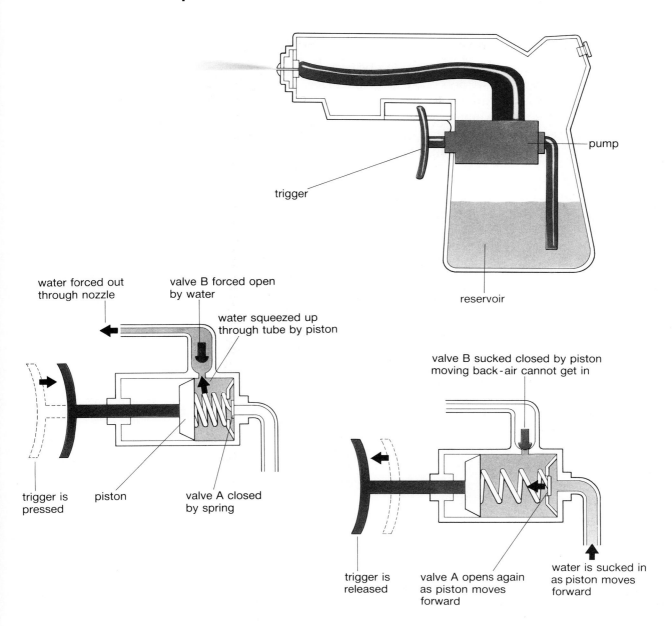

pump

trigger

reservoir

water forced out through nozzle

valve B forced open by water

water squeezed up through tube by piston

trigger is pressed

piston

valve A closed by spring

valve B sucked closed by piston moving back - air cannot get in

trigger is released

valve A opens again as piston moves forward

water is sucked in as piston moves forward

Writing

Explain in your own words how a water-pistol works.

Run for your life

It was a rainy day in November when I met him first, and about a regiment of them seemed to be bashing him. He was a little dark skinny kid who looked about eight, but I knew he couldn't be because of the school cap. It was our school cap, and we don't take kids under eleven. The cap was in a puddle, and so was this kid. He was down on his knees in it, and that's where they were bashing him.

As far as I could see, he was letting them. He wasn't struggling or yelling or anything. He was just kneeling there sobbing, and doing that pretty quietly.

I said, 'All right, break it up.'

It was dark in the alley and they had to peer at me.

'Get lost,' one of them said, uncertainly.

'Yeah, vanish.'

'Scramaroo.'

They let go of him all the same.

I could see they were younger than me, and smaller, which was all right except one of them had some kind of cosh in his hand, a piece of hosepipe or something.

'I know you!' this one yelled suddenly, just about the same moment I realised I knew him, too. He was a tough young kid with an elder brother who'd made my life a misery at another school. 'You're Woolcott, ain't you? I know where you live, Woolcott. Better shove off if you don't want trouble.'

'Yeah, shove.'

'Buzz off. He's ours.'

I said to the kid, 'Get up.'

'You leave him alone,' the kid with the cosh said. 'He started it. He hit one of us.'

'Yeah, he was throwing things.'

'Were you throwing things?' I said to the kid.

He just shook his head, still sobbing.

'Yes, you did, you rotten little liar! He caught Harris, didn't he, Harris?'

'Right here,' Harris said, pointing to his temple. 'I've still got a headache.'

I said, 'What did he throw?'

'He threw a ball. He threw it flipping hard, too. We was in the timber yard and he run away before we could see who done it.'

'How do you know it was him, then?'

'He told us,' Harris said triumphantly. 'He come up and laughed and told us right out, didn't he?'

'Yeah.'

'Yeah, right out, he did. He done it last Thursday and he come up just now and said it was him. Laughing, too.'

'I only asked for my ball back,' the kid said. It was the first time he'd spoken, and I looked at him twice because it was with a foreign accent. 'I saw them playing with it and I came up and apologized and asked for it back. It was only an accident. I didn't mean to hit anybody. It went over the wall by mistake.'

'Yeah, you rotten little liar, you threw it.'

'No, please, I didn't. It's the only ball I've got.'

'The only one you had. . .'

I said, 'Give him his ball back.'

'You take a jump.'

'Give him it back, quick.'

They were ganging up round me, and the one with the cosh was fingering it, so I made a quick snatch before he was ready and got it off him.

I said, 'Give him his ball.'

One of them pulled a ball out of his pocket and dropped it on the ground, and the kid picked it up.

'My brother'll murder you,' the kid with the brother said.

'Give him his satchel, too.'

'He'll jump about on you. He'll tear you in little pieces. He'll give you such a crunching —'

I said, 'If those are your bikes jump on them quick.'

Their bikes were leaning up against the alley wall and they got on them and pushed off.

'I wouldn't like to be you,' the kid with the brother said.

He said something else, too, but I didn't catch it. They were all laughing as they rode off.

I picked up the kid's cap from the puddle and stuck it on his head.

I said, 'You're a bit of a case, aren't you? What do you want to tell them you did it for?'

'They had my ball,' the kid said, still sobbing. 'I thought they might hit me, but they ought to give it back.'

'Give it back! Look, you want to keep away from that lot,' I said. 'They'd do you up just for fun. Risk a good hiding for a rotten old ball you can buy anywhere for ninepence?'

'I haven't got ninepence,' the kid said. 'I only get threepence a week. My mother can't afford any more.'

I said, 'All right, then, come on,' a bit embarrassed, and hoping he'd dry up now.

He didn't dry up. He started telling me his life story.

I said, 'Look, you don't have to tell me all this.'

'That's all right. I like to tell you.'

He said he was Hungarian and his family had had to run away from there. His father had died about a year ago and his mother was having a hard time earning money. He was still going on about it when we got to the end of the street, and I saw with relief — because at least it shut him up

– that the gang hadn't gone home yet. They were waiting for us, circling on their bikes. They had lumps of mud.

We got our heads down and ran. The kid still managed to cop a couple down the back of the neck before we got to his gate.

I said, 'You'd better tidy up a bit, hadn't you, before you go in?'

'Yes. Thank you.'

He was pushing something in my hand, and I thought he wanted me to hold it while he wiped his neck.

He said shyly, 'It's a present. I want you to have it.'

I looked in my hand and saw three pennies and nearly went up the wall. I said, 'Here, I don't want it.'

'Please. It's for you.'

'I don't want it.'

I tried to give it back, but his hand wasn't there and the pennies went rolling in the gutter. He gave a sort of gulp and turned away, and just then I remembered it was all his spending money and he'd given it to me. So I got down and found it.

'Here. Put it in your pocket.'

'It's for you.'

'Come on.' I forced it in his pocket.

'I'm sorry,' he said. 'I don't know how you do things. I haven't any friends here . . . Forgive me.'

He looked so weird I said, 'All right, forget it. What's your name, anyway?'

'Szolda,' he said. 'Istvan Szolda.'

It sounded like Soldier the way he said it, so I said, 'Okay, Soldier – see you again.'

His face came whipping round, smiling all over as if I'd given him the best present he could think of.

'Oh, yes, please. Thank you, Woolcott,' he said.

I suppose I was hooked from then on.

David Line *Run For Your Life*

Questions

1   What was happening at the beginning of the story?
2   Who is telling the story?
3   Why do you think he stops and gets involved?
4   Why were the gang picking on 'Soldier'?
5   What had really happened?
6   Who was 'Soldier'?
7   What impression do you get of him from reading the story?
8   Why do you think the story-teller decided to help him?
9   How do you think the story might continue?

Writing

Think about your answer to the last question. Now write your version of what happens next.

Flood!

Imagine that your school is flooded suddenly!
The nearby river has burst its banks and the
water is rushing through the school. You do
not have much time to think. You know that
you must move quickly – UPWARDS.

**Think: Which is the highest point of the
school?**

From the classroom you are in, which is the
quickest way to get there?

Can you get out on to the roof easily?

The water has rushed through the building so
rapidly that only six of you have made your
escape. Perhaps you were all quick-thinking,
or strong, or agile, or just lucky.

Your companions

1   Make a list of the six who have escaped.
    (They can be real people, or people you
    have made up.)
2   Alongside each name, say why that
    person was able to get out safely. (There
    may be more than one reason for each
    person.)

Describing your escape

1   Describe how you escape on to the roof.
2   Draw a map showing the route you took.

From the roof you can see into some of the classrooms.

As the classroom floods

Write about someone in one of these rooms, from just before s/he knew of the danger until the time that the water overwhelmed the room. Remember to write about what the person saw and heard, as well as what s/he thought and felt.

Spend some time thinking about a good title for this piece of writing.

Who will be saved and why?

Luckily for you, today was the day of the annual school fair. A demonstration of hot-air ballooning was to have been part of the entertainment. The balloon is on the roof, where it was placed early in the morning, for use later in the day. You can escape!
You need to move quite quickly because the water is still rising.

Unfortunately, the balloon will only hold **three** people.

1 How would you decide which three should be saved?
2 Who would be chosen?
3 Write an account of what happened as the flood waters rose and the three people were chosen.

The area around your school is now completely flooded.

Seen from above

You are one of the three people in the balloon.

Preparation

Think:

1 What do you see?
2 What do you hear?
3 Are there any signs of life?
4 What **permanent** damage has been done?
5 Will it be possible for life to return to normal in the future? If so, how?

Writing

Describe in detail the scene below you and your thoughts as you look down and think about the future.

Suddenly you notice that the water is coming nearer. The balloon is dropping fast. It looks as if your luck has run out! We are told that when we are in great danger, different events of our lives go through our minds.

Thoughts

Preparation

1 Which is the most important event of your life: the one you would remember first?
2 Which person, or people, would you think of first?

Writing

Now write the thoughts that rush through your mind as the balloon begins to fall.

40

You decide that the balloon is too heavy with three people on board. One person will have to go! It is not likely to be you, is it? You and the remaining person will 'help' the third one out of the balloon.

Who will it be?

Preparation

1   Which person would you choose to go over the side?
2   Why would you choose that person?

Writing

Describe how you decided and then what happened.

Sadly, the balloon continues to drop, but more slowly now. The balloon is still too heavy. Someone else must go, too. It looks as if you are going to be left alone! But before that, you must convince your partner that you deserve to be saved; or, perhaps, that s/he will enjoy the swim.

The argument

In script form, write the argument between you and your partner about which of you is to stay in the balloon. End with one of you 'leaving'.

What is real courage?

The mountaineer
- Always looking for new challenges.
- Facing danger on every new route.
- Willing to take risks most of us would find terrifying.

The racing driver
- Dicing with death in every Grand Prix.
- Showing driving skill and nerve as he takes a bend or overtakes with only inches to spare.
- Accidents mean broken bones, horrible burns, death.

The relief worker
- Working in the poorest countries of the world, bringing help to the starving and sick.
- Facing disease, discomfort, and even attack.
- Paid very little despite her training and experience.

The fireman
- Always on call to fight fire.
- Facing danger from fire, smoke, falling buildings.
- Saving other people's lives at risk to his own.

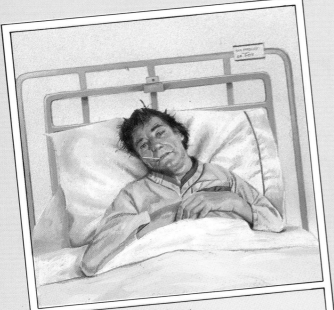

The hospital patient
- Daily suffering pain and discomfort.
- Never complaining but always having a cheerful word and a smile.
- Facing serious illness bravely.

The sub-postmistress
- Was attacked by thugs demanding money, but refused to give in.
- Drove off the thugs with a broomstick.
- Suffered serious head-injuries in the attack and had to stop working.

These are all people who have been admired for their courage. Read carefully what it says about each one. Do you admire them? Are they all equally brave? Do you admire some more than others? If so, why? Think about them, and then answer these questions.

Making a choice

Each of these people shows courage, but in different ways.

1. For each one explain how that person shows courage.
2. Which one do you admire most and why?
3. Which do you admire least and why?

Writing

Choose three of the people to write about. For each one:

1. Write a short description of his/her life and achievements based on the notes.
2. Write an explanation of why you have chosen him/her.

Something to think about

Each of these people is admired and thought to be brave. You probably think some are better than others.

1. Why is this?
2. Are some kinds of courage better than others?
3. If so, which kinds are better and why?
4. When do you have to show courage in your own life?

43

MYSTERY HEROES

Brave youths disappear after saving policeman

POLICE in Gloucester are still puzzling over the behaviour of two brave young men. These mystery heroes saved a police officer from serious injury in an incident at Gloucester Docks yesterday. But when he recovered enough to thank them, his rescuers had vanished.

PC George Davis was on beat duty in the Docks area at 7.30 p.m. last Tuesday. He noticed that a door had been broken open in one of the warehouses. As he approached, two men came out carrying an item of furniture. He asked them what they were doing and was then attacked.

Sorting out what happened

The newspaper report gives us all the facts of the story, but it doesn't tell them in the order in which they happened.

1 Write down the main points of the story.
2 Make sure that you have written them in the order in which they happened.
3 Make a list of the names, or descriptions, of all the people mentioned.
4 Is there anything you would like to know about the story which isn't mentioned? If so, make a list of questions you would like to ask.

Questions to think about

1 What is your opinion of the behaviour of the people who helped the police?
2 You are walking along a street near your home. You see a policeman being attacked by two men. What things can you possibly do? Make a list of them. What would be the most sensible thing to do and why?

Now read the newspaper report on page 45.

What is your opinion?

Here are three short pieces of conversation about the people described in the two newspaper cuttings. Read each one and then explain what you think.

Mystery heroes

A: I think it's magnificent, standing up to those thugs like that.
B: I don't. They need their heads testing. Look after number one, that's what I say.

Here's to you, lovely little Lisa

BRISTOL schoolgirl Lisa Cummings has been named as one of this year's Children of Achievement for the courage she showed in coping with cancer.

Lisa, 14 (pictured), of Somerset Avenue, Chipping Sodbury, was diagnosed as having cancer two years ago and had to have an operation to remove a tumour from her leg. Then she was put on a chemo-therapy course which made all her hair fall out.

But despite this Lisa remained cheerful and carried on going to school. She kept up with her school work and her trumpet playing throughout her ordeal.

Her mother Ann Cummings said: "I wasn't surprised by her courage — she has never been a moaner. But we were totally surprised by the award because we didn't even know she'd been entered."

Lisa was recommended for the award by her headmistress at Red Maid's school in Westbury-on-Trym, Miss Enid Castle.

Miss Castle said: "I thought she deserved the award because she has been very brave and had to cope with the cancer operation and all the nasty bits that go with it.

"She is a very pleasant and lively girl."

Lisa, who is now in good health, collected the award, which is sponsored by Sesame Travel, at a ceremony at London's Guildhall on Tuesday.

● Jill Graham, 15, from Hart-cliffe was also presented with an award for looking after her mother, Wendy, who has to use a dialysis machine for five hours at a time because of kidney failure. Jill was rec-ommended for the award by her deputy headmistress Mrs Lena Rust from Hartcliffe Comprehensive School.

A: What — and leave the policeman to be beaten up?

B: They're paid to face danger — that's their problem.

Lisa Cummings

A: Isn't she brave!

B: I can't see what all the fuss is about. If you're ill you're ill. It hasn't got anything to do with courage.

Jill Graham

B: So she looked after her mother. What's so wonderful about that?

A: Her mother is an invalid. She has to help her **and** help with the house **and** go to school.

B: Big deal!

A: I'd like to see you do all that and stay cheerful. That takes real guts.

45

A long story

In the last two units you have been thinking about settings and characters for your stories. Now you can try to write a long story of your own.

What am I going to write about?

You may have thought of a good subject for your story while you were working on characters and settings. If so, there's no problem. If not, here is a suggestion. Have another look at the newspaper cutting on page 44. It contains a mystery:

Who were the boys who helped PC Davis?
Where did they come from?
Where did they go to?
Why did they run away?
Will they go to the police to be thanked?

Think about these boys. Make them the main characters of a story. Think about where they live and where the fight happened. Think about why they helped and even more important, their secret reasons for running away afterwards. You can make it all up in your head, or you can use some of the material opposite to help you.

Organising your story

1   Do your thinking.
2   Write a rough version of your story.
3   Think about ways of making it better.*
4   Do a final version.

*There are ideas about this in the unit called *Drafting* on pages 112–15.

Dauntless Little John

There was once a lad whom everyone called Dauntless Little John, since he was afraid of nothing. Travelling about the world, he came to an inn, where he asked for lodgings. 'We have no room here,' said the innkeeper, 'but if you're not afraid, I will direct you to a certain palace where you can stay.'

'Why should I be afraid?'

'People shudder at the thought of that palace, since nobody who's gone in has come out alive. In the morning friars go up with the bier* for anyone brave enough to spend the night inside.'

So what did Little John do but pick up a lamp, a bottle, and a sausage, and march straight to the palace.

At midnight he was sitting at the table eating, when he heard a voice in the chimney. 'Shall I throw it down?'

'Go ahead!' replied Little John.

Down the chimney into the fireplace fell a man's leg. Little John drank a glass of wine.

Then the voice spoke again. 'Shall I throw it down?'

'Go ahead!' So another leg dropped into the fireplace. Little John bit into the sausage.

'Shall I throw it down?'

'Go ahead!' So down came an arm. Little John began whistling a tune.

'Shall I throw it down?'

'By all means!' And there was another arm.

'Shall I throw it down?'

'Yes!'

Then came the trunk of a body, and the arms and legs stuck onto it, and there stood a man without a head.

'Shall I throw it down?'

'Throw it down!'

Down came the head and sprang into place atop the trunk. He was truly a giant, and Little John raised his glass and said, 'To your health!'

The giant said, 'Take up the lamp and come with me.'

Little John picked up the lamp, but didn't budge.

'You go first,' said the giant.

'No, after you,' insisted Little John.

'After you!' thundered the giant.

'You lead the way!' yelled Little John.

So the giant went first, with Little John behind him lighting the way, and they went through room after room until they had walked the whole length of the palace. Beneath one of the staircases was a small door.

'Open it!' ordered the giant.

'You open it!' replied Little John.

So the giant shoved it open with his shoulder. There was a spiral staircase.

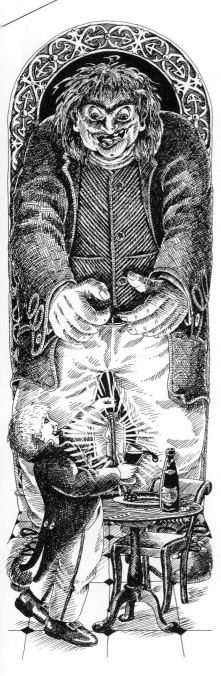

bier stretcher for
a corpse

48

'Go on down,' directed the giant.

'After you,' answered Little John.

They went down the steps into a cellar, and the giant pointed to a stone slab on the ground. 'Raise that!'

'You raise it!' replied Little John, and the giant lifted it as though it were a mere pebble.

Beneath the slab were three pots of gold. 'Carry those upstairs!' ordered the giant.

'You carry them up!' answered Little John. And the giant carried them up one by one.

When they were back in the hall where the great fireplace was, the giant said, 'Little John, the spell has been broken!' At that one of his legs came off and kicked its way up the chimney. 'One of these pots of gold is for you.' An arm came loose and climbed up the chimney. 'The second pot of gold is for the friars who come to carry away your body, believing you perished.' The other arm came off and followed the first. 'The third pot of gold is for the first poor man who comes by.' Then the other leg dropped off, leaving the giant seated on the floor. 'Keep the palace for yourself.' The trunk separated from the head and vanished. 'The owners of the palace and their children are now gone forever.' At that the head disappeared up the chimney.

As soon as it was light, a dirge arose: *Miserere mei, miserere mei.** The friars had come with the bier to carry off Little John's body. But there he stood, at the window, smoking his pipe!

Dauntless Little John was a wealthy youth indeed with all those gold pieces, and he lived happily in his palace. Then one day what should he do but look behind him and see his shadow: he was so frightened, he died.

Italo Calvino   *Italian Folk Tales*   ** Miserere mei* Have mercy upon me

A radio play

This story would make a good radio play. You don't even have to write it down. All you do is this:

1   You need a group of four readers:
    A   Dauntless Little John
    B   The story-teller
    C   The giant
    D   The other speakers
2   Go through the story, working out who says what. For example, the beginning works like this:

B: There was once a lad whom everyone called Dauntless Little John, since he was afraid of nothing. Travelling about the world, he came to an inn, where he asked for lodgings.
D: We have no room here.
B: Said the innkeeper.
D: But if you're not afraid, I will direct you to a certain palace where you can stay.
A: Why should I be afraid?
3   Now practise reading the story until you are satisfied with your play.

49

Poems about courage and fear

Camping out

His birthday fell in mid-July,
A golden season filled with trees,
Green cauldrons bubbling in the sky
With songs of birds, and, on the breeze
Like airborne petals, butterflies
Signalled, 'Peter now is nine!'

That morning brought a great surprise
Which sent a thrill along his spine
And filled his heart with wordless joy:
His parents gave to him a tent,
A gift that almost any boy
Would welcome, but to him it meant
A dream had wakened into fact —
For months he'd longed to spend a night
Under canvas; all he lacked
Had in a second been put right
When he unpacked his birthday present.
'I'll camp in Coppin's field tonight.'
His father smiled: 'It sounds quite pleasant.
But Peter, out there in the dark
You might be frightened, all alone.
Just now the whole thing seems a lark
But night has terrors of its own.'
Peter laughed and said he knew
That night and day were different;
He felt no fear of darkness. So
          As evening fell he pitched his tent
          And climbed into his sleeping-bag.
          The sun slipped down the West's red throat
          And soon the skies began to sag
          With weight of blackness, noises float
          Eerily in night's dark lake;

Sounds he could not recognize,
Sounds of menace, made him shake,
Sounds that put on strange disguise
As this prowling darkness thickened,
Sounds suggesting hideous forms
Groaned and sighed as heart-beat quickened
Sounds that spoke of giant worms,
Vampires, demons, scaly beasts.
Peter soon could bear no more;
With chattering teeth he dressed in haste,
Peered once into the dark before
He plunged into the night to flee
On stumbling feet with gasp and moan
Towards the sweet security
That beckoned from his lighted home.
Next day he visited that site
Of freezing horror, but he saw
Nothing of the shapes of night;
The grass was innocent once more,
The petal dance of butterflies
Winked and twinkled, birdsong thrilled
The grateful silence: earth and skies
Wore festive dress, while flowers filled
The air with fragrance and delight;
Each breath he drew seemed like a kiss.
The boy could scarce believe that this
Was where black dread had stalked at night.
Then, dimly, he began to see
That demons, ghosts, and gnomes, and elves
Are necessary fictions we
Mentally create ourselves:
Most monsters die exposed to light
Outside the dark world of the head.
But, all the same, he'd spend tonight
Safe in his warm, familiar bed.

Vernon Scannell

Blind boy on the shore

Set down by himself on the sandy shore,
Unseeing, as if asleep.
He dug at once with his new spade;
And, heap after little heap,

He filled and emptied his pail, groping
Each time with steady hand,
And sensitive fingers' touch, to test
The shape of the moulded sand.

But little by little his work slackened;
He sat with uplifted spade,
And listened instead to the far sea,
And the cries of children who played.

Then, from close by, there came the quiet
Singing of a younger child...
He dug no more, but gave up gently,
Lay back in the sun, and smiled.

John Walsh

Thinking about the poems

1   Peter was nine. Do you think he was a
    coward?
2   In what way is the blind boy showing
    courage?
3   At the end of the poem, why does the
    blind boy smile?
4   Can you think of occasions in your life,
    like **Camping out**, when you knew you
    would be frightened but still insisted on
    having your own way? What happened
    in the end?
5   We could say that the blind boy has a
    kind of **quiet** courage. Can you think of
    other examples of this kind of courage?

Your writing

Being brave often means that you have to
overcome your own fear to do something you
think is important or worthwhile. Think of a
story about someone who is faced with just
this kind of challenge. S/he really is frightened
to start with, but has to try to overcome that
fear. Decide what happens in the end: does it
work, or does fear win? When you have
decided, write your story.

The telescope poem

Imagine you are looking through a telescope. You are able to zoom in on smaller and smaller details of the scene. Each line of your poem brings us closer and closer to the main subject. The last line should be more thoughtful.

Through my telescope I can see a town

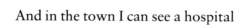

And in the town I can see a hospital

In the hospital I can see a window

And through the window I can see a ward

In the ward I can see a bed
And in the bed an old man sleeps:

He is dreaming of peace and days
without pain.

Here is another telescope poem:

Through my telescope I can see a park
And in the park there's an adventure
playground
In the playground I can see a death-slide
And at the top of it I can see a boy
He is looking down and clinging on with both
hands
In his eyes is a look of fear:

I wonder what he's frightened of.

Now you try

A   Here is the outline of a telescope poem.
Copy it out and fill in the missing words.

Through my telescope I can see a house
And on the house I can see a roof
On the _____ I can see _____
And on _____ I can see _____
Now I can see that _____
_____
_____

B   Now make up your own telescope poem.
Here are some first lines you could use:

Through my telescope I can see a school
Through my telescope I can see a beach
Through my telescope I can see a crowd
Through my telescope I can see a garden

A variation

C   Now try writing a poem which does the
opposite to the telescope poem. It begins
with a close up and moves away to
describe the scene all around like the
pictures on the right.

Break-in

It is early one Monday morning. Police have been called to a small railway station, where there has been a break-in during the weekend, some time between 9.30 p.m. on Saturday and 6.00 a.m. on Monday.

You are the detective on the case. Pictured below is what you see when you arrive. You are told that the safe is missing.

Your investigation

Work out the answers to these questions.

1   How did the thief, or thieves, get into the building?
2   Is this usual? If not, why not?
3   How were the thieves able to see?
4   Is this usual? If not, why not?
5   What does the broken penknife tell you?
6   Where do you think the safe was? Why?
7   What has happened to the safe? What proof have you of this?
8   How many people took part in the break-in, do you think? Why?

Your notes

At each stage in the investigation you have to make brief notes describing:

1   What you have seen.
2   What you have worked out.

Write your notes.

Your investigation

1 Why do the tracks not lead to the car park?
2 Do these pictures tell you any more about the sort of person, or people, who have broken in?

More clues

You follow the marks down the line until they stop, and new marks take their place. These are two marks, side by side, each about fourteen centimetres wide and about one metre apart.

Your investigation

Have a clear idea what the new tracks are like. Measure them out on your desk or on the floor.

Another break-in

You can see that the new tracks stop at a gate about 100 metres along the line. As you set off towards the gate, a man shouts and comes towards you across a field. You know the man. He is a window-cleaner.

Your investigation

1 What do you think has happened?
2 Does this tell you any more about the thief, or thieves?
3 From this new evidence, have you a better idea of **when** the crime was committed?

Your notes

Now write your notes.

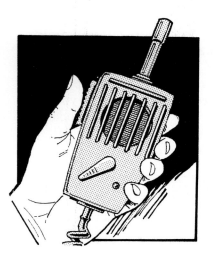

At this point you receive a message on your personal radio from the local police station.

These are the questions they ask you. The trouble is that they have got jumbled up:

- What are you going to do now?
- Do you think it will be long before we can make an arrest?
- Was it a professional job, then?
- Would there be much money in it?
- Where are you at the moment?

Sorting it out

1 Work out the order the questions should be in.
2 Work out your answers to them.
3 Write the conversation (including your replies) as a script.

After the radio message, you follow the marks through the gate by the railway line. They lead past some farm buildings and across two fields, through more gates. The marks are easy to follow. In the third field, by the hedge, you find exactly what you have expected to find.

Your investigation

1 Think about the clues so far.
2 Make notes on what you have found.
3 Draw a picture of what you see in the field, by the hedge.

You will now call in the fingerprint experts. However, you should have some idea of the sort of person, or persons, you are looking for.

Look carefully at what you have written so far, and look again at the evidence.

Think about these questions:
- Had the break-in been planned?
- What do you already **know** about who did it?

Your report

Copy out and fill in the report form below. It is for your Inspector. In the first part you will need to describe carefully what you have seen. In the second part, give your thoughts and the reasons for them.

Use your notes to help you fill it in.

Westlea Police	OFFICIAL REPORT
Date:	Place: *Westlea Railway Station*
Crime: *Break-in and Robbery*	

Details of the scene of the crime:	Comments on the evidence:

Signed:	Detective Sergeant

The confession

You interview the people whom you suspect. One of them breaks down under questioning. S/he confesses everything. Write the confession. (You should write as 'I' and include all the details.)

Comics and magazines

Who reads these?

1 Which of these comics and magazines have you read?
2 Do you read any of them at the moment?
3 Pick the odd one out in each column, and explain why it is the odd one out.

4 Make a list of comics and magazines which are read by people of your age, and which are not shown here.
5 Now organise your list into groups according to type of comic or magazine.

Column A	Column B	Column C	Column D

What's your favourite comic or magazine?

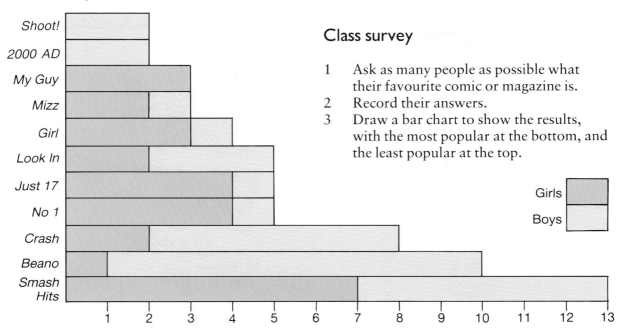

Class survey

1 Ask as many people as possible what their favourite comic or magazine is.
2 Record their answers.
3 Draw a bar chart to show the results, with the most popular at the bottom, and the least popular at the top.

Questions

Look at the bar chart and answer these questions:

1 Which magazine or comic was most popular with girls?
2 Which magazine or comic was most popular with boys?
3 How many girls voted for Crash?
4 What was the vote for Just 17?

Detailed report

1 Choose a favourite comic or magazine.
2 Copy out the questionnaire on the right.
3 Fill in the answers. You will find this much easier if you have the comic or magazine in front of you.

Questionnaire

a What is the title?
b What is the price?
c Is it for boys, girls, or both sexes?
d What age-group is it for?
e What **type** of publication is it? (e.g. fun comic, pop magazine, etc.)
f What interests do its readers have?
g What kinds of thing does it contain?
h What kind of pictures does it contain?
i Are there any colour pages in it, or are they all black and white?
j If it contains stories, are they mainly real life or fantasy?
k Is there a typical hero/heroine? If so what is s/he like?
l Is there a typical baddie/villain? If so what is s/he like?
m What kinds of product are advertised in the magazine?
n How could the magazine or comic be improved?
o Is it good value for money? Why?

Picture stories

Comparing the two

Study the picture stories on these two pages. The speech bubbles have been deliberately blanked out. Answer these questions about each of the stories. Every time you make an answer try to give the reasons for your answer.

1. What sort of comic or magazine does the story come from?
2. What sort of reader is it meant for?
3. Describe the main characters. How are we expected to think about them?
4. How would you expect the story to continue?
5. Each of the speech bubbles is lettered. Write down the words that you think should go in each one.

"I'm not going to take sides."

Graham's disco plans have been wrecked by a double-booking at a local hall. Meanwhile Arthur has been having a go at Clare for coming in late.

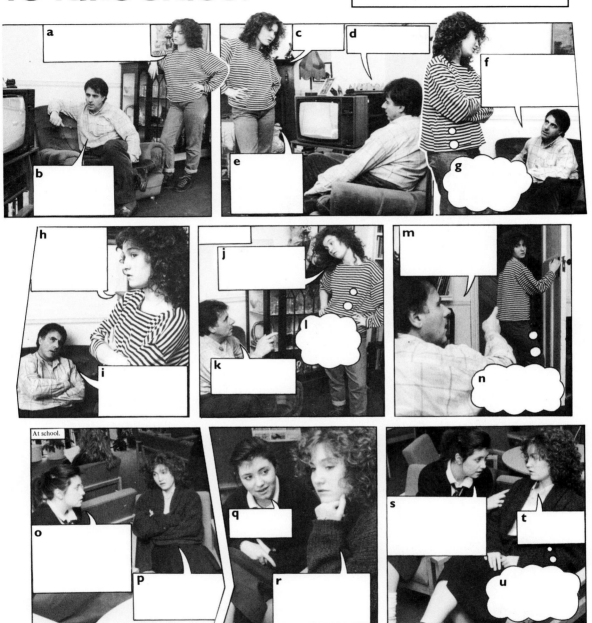

Writing a different version

Now imagine a completely different version of each story, but with the same pictures. Make each character the opposite of what you think they are meant to be like: heroes become villains and villains become heroes. Write down the words you would put in the speech bubbles now.

Making a story-line

1 Choose one of the pairs of characters to work on.
2 Decide where the story takes place.
3 Decide whether your story is going to be serious, or whether you are going to send the whole thing up.
4 Decide how long your story will be:
　　How many pictures altogether?
　　How many to a page?

Name: Pagos　　*Home:* planet Zythos

Lord of the Mighty Forces and chief enemy of the Golden Champions, the governors of the universe. He commands the Zythonoids, robot warriors who are almost indestructible.

Name: Helos　　*Home:* Earth

Captain of the Golden Champions' Defence Force. Her task is to prevent Pagos from overthrowing the chosen governors of the universe. So far she has been successful, but will Pagos and the Zythonoids win this time?

5 Write down the outline of your story.
6 Decide on the important moments: the ones that will be illustrated.
7 Work out what will go in each picture.
8 Work out the words you need:
   in speech bubbles,
   underneath the pictures, telling the story.
9 Draw the frames for the pictures.
10 Start drawing the pictures.

Name: Mandy   *Age:* 15
She has known Geoff for three months but recently she has been irritated by his selfishness and lack of consideration for others.

Name: Geoff   *Age:* 16
He has a high opinion of himself. He has just left school but doesn't know what he wants to do. He's never really thought about his feelings for Mandy.

£25,750
Detached, two-bedroomed residence.
Central position, close to public transport. Suit DIY enthusiast.

Nothing but the truth?

So what's wrong?

This advertisement is **true but misleading**.

1 Copy out and complete this table.
2 Now explain briefly why the advertisement can be described as true but misleading.

What it says	The truth
Detached, two-bedroomed residence	
Central position	

S REG FAMILY CAR One owner from new. Good mileage. Must be seen to be believed. Needs some attention. — Telephone 276894

Suppose that this car was advertised by the same person who was trying to sell the house in the advertisement on page 64. What do you think the car would really look like?

1 Describe the car in detail.
2 Now write an advertisement by the same person, who wants to sell one of the things in the pictures below.

Brian Walker

What about these?

In what ways might each of the following advertisements be misleading?

1 **Come to sunny Sludgeville. A great time guaranteed.**

2 **Book your holidays at Clacksea, where the sun always shines.**

3 **Shop at Tescbury's for the lowest prices in town.**

4 **Tony's restaurant: the best value for miles around.**

5 **Heavy jobs around the house? Don't kill your husband – let us do it.**

6 **Julian's salon: hundreds of satisfied customers – They know no better.**

Problem page

The editor of **Hi There!** magazine often receives letters from readers with problems. Sometimes she publishes these letters in the magazine along with her replies, which give advice on how to solve the problems. Unfortunately she's had a few problems herself recently and has not been doing her job very well. All the letters and her replies to them are put on the office computer. One day the editor pressed the wrong key and jumbled two letters up completely. Then she got the replies she had written completely jumbled up, too.

The letters

```
There are some boys around my way who pick on anyone they feel
like annoying, and at the moment it's my brother. I just can't
afford it. I was really pleased at first but now I've found I'm
meant to pay for my own dress and she's chosen a very expensive
one. When I saw them doing it, I had a go at them, and now
they're calling me names. It's really upsetting him because
they push him and jeer at him. A cousin of mine is getting
married and has asked me to be a bridesmaid. What can I do ?
What should I do ?
```

The answers

If you do this, I'm sure that after a while when they see it doesn't bother you, they'll stop. As she's expecting you to pay for the dress, she should have discussed with you how much you could afford beforehand. The best thing to do is just ignore them. Then tell her what you can afford to pay. And perhaps if your brother continues to have trouble with them, you should advise him to do the same. I don't think your cousin's being very fair here. I know this might be hard, but when they start, just walk away and pretend that you can't hear them. Get on the phone to her and explain that you can't afford the dress she's chosen and you're as disappointed as she is about it. Believe me, they'll soon get fed up. This way she can either put some money towards the dress herself to cover the difference, or look for something in the right price range. It was good of you to stand up for him but he has got to learn to fight his own battles - unless of course he's much younger than you are.

What to do

1 Sort out the two letters and write them out separately.
2 Sort out the two answers and write them out.

Word square

This square contains the names of twelve newspapers and magazines. The words read across, forwards or backwards, vertically, up or down and diagonally, forwards or backwards. Some of them consist of two words, *without* a space between them.

```
N N A T I L O P O M S O C X S
U D R P P Z U M G L G O N T U
S R A N Y E L L Q U U R W Z N
A N D I M S O W N Y A F O O D
T T I A L E M P I C R O S E A
U Q O T N Y L S L N D O N S Y
R A T E T S T N E E I W A S T
M F I R M O T E H E A M M I I
D L M D E E S A L T N P O R M
G A E R N T E I D E I S W E E
A N S A D M A I T H G S T H S
T D W I H M E B S S A R W E H
H E I R A N G A T E S C A A N
E X P R E S S T T O N L A P P
R U E S A Y R O R R I M S E H
```

In brief

Some newspaper headlines can be very confusing.

Javed's 153

This could mean that it is the birthday of a very old man. In fact, of course, it tells us how many runs a batsman has scored.

Johnson at number 10

This could mean:

1 Johnson has become Prime Minister.
2 Johnson has visited the Prime Minister.
3 Johnson has made a record which is selling well.

Fire brigade put out

This could mean:

1 The fire brigade is upset about something.
2 The fire brigade has been turned out of somewhere.
3 The fire brigade has burst into flames and had to be hosed down.

Javed's 153

Johnson at number 10

Fire brigade put out

Now explain these

Think of as many different meanings as you can for each of the headlines.

'That's life' says Judge

Ex mayor down in the dumps

Pickets hit buses

Tell the story

Some headlines are easier to understand. **In one sentence each** tell the story behind these headlines:

MISSING WOMAN FOUND
Remembers nothing

PLANE CRASH INQUIRY
Faulty panel blamed

ESCAPE BID FAILS
Balloon hits pylon

Make up the headline

For each of the following news items make up a suitable headline.

1 Hope faded today for the five circus animals trapped in a building which collapsed last night after being hit by a large pylon blown down by high winds.
2 Recent scientific discoveries have suggested that women who eat a lot of cabbages live longer than normal.
3 The government has announced that from next year it will provide special facilities in motorway service areas for people who are physically handicapped.

Now make up headlines for these two news photographs.

69

Equal rights

'Can't you read?'

The man was looking at me and reaching under the counter as if he was going for his gun. He came up with another one of his signs to spread over the front of a paper.

'"Only two children at a time allowed in this shop,"' he read out, loudly.

I looked across at the the two kids in the corner. They were pretending to pick penny chews while they gawped at the girls on the magazines. OK, I made three, but I wasn't there for the same reason as them. Couldn't he recognise business when he saw it?

'I'm not buying,' I said, 'I've come about the job.'

He frowned at me, in between watching the boys in the corner. 'What job?' he said. He was all on edge with three of us in the shop.

'Reliable paper-boy wanted.' I told him. 'Enquire within.'

'Hurry up, you two!' he shouted. And then he frowned at me again as if I was something from outer space.

'But you're not a boy,' he said. '"Reliable paper-*boy* required," that says. If I'd meant "boy *or girl*" I'd have put it on, wouldn't I? Or "paper-*person*!"' He did this false laugh for the benefit of a man with a briefcase standing at the counter.

'Oh,' I said, disappointed. 'Only I'm *reliable*, that's all. I get up early with my dad, I'm never off school, and I can tell the difference between the *Sun* and the *Beano*.'

'I'm glad someone can,' the man with the briefcase said.

But the paper-man didn't laugh. He was looking at me, hard.

'Where d'you live?' he asked.

'Round the corner.'

'Could you start at seven?'

'Six, if you like.'

'Rain or shine, winter and summer?'

'No problem.' I stared at him, and he stared at me. He looked as if he was deciding whether or not to give women the vote.

'All right,' he said, 'I'll give you a chance. Start Monday. Seven o'clock, do your own marking-up. Four pounds a week, plus Christmas tips. Two weeks' holiday without pay . . .'

Now that he'd made up his mind he smiled at me, overdoing the big favour.

'Is that what the boys get?' I asked. 'Four pounds a week?'

He started unwrapping a packet of fags. 'I don't see how that concerns you. The money suits or it doesn't. Four pounds is what I said, and four pounds is what I meant. Take it or leave it.' He looked at Briefcase again, shaking his head at the cheek of the girl.

I walked back to the door. 'I'll leave it, then,' I said, 'seeing the boys get five pounds, *and* a week's holiday with pay.' I knew all this because Jason used to do it. 'Thanks anyway, I'll tell my dad what you said . . .'

'Please yourself.'

I slammed out of the shop. I was mad, I can tell you. Cheap labour, he was after: thought he was on to a good thing for a minute, you could tell that.

The trouble was, I really needed a bit of money coming in, saving for those shoes and things I wanted. There was no way I'd get them otherwise. But I wasn't going to be treated any different from the boys. I wouldn't have a shorter round or lighter papers, would I? Everything'd be the same, except the money.

I walked the long way home, thinking. It was nowhere near Guy Fawkes, and carol singing was even further away. So that really only left car washing – and they leave the rain to wash the cars round our way.

Hearing this baby cry gave me the idea. Without thinking about it I knocked at the door where the bawling was coming from.

The lady opened it and stared at me like you stare at double glazing salesmen, when you're cross for being brought to the door.

'Baby-play calling,' I said, making up the name from somewhere.

The lady said, 'Eh?' and she looked behind me to see who was pulling my strings.

'Baby-play,' I said. 'We come and play with your baby in your own home. Keep it happy. Or walk it out, not going across main roads.'

She opened the door a bit wider. The baby crying got louder.

'How much?' she asked.

That really surprised me. I'd felt sorry about calling from the first lift of the knocker, and here she was taking me seriously.

'I don't know,' I said. 'Whatever you think . . .'

'Well . . .' She looked at me to see if she'd seen me before; to see if I was local enough to be trusted. Then I was glad I had the school jumper on, so she knew I could be traced. 'You push Bobby down the shops and get Mr Dawson's magazines, and I'll give you twenty pence. Take your time, mind...'

'All right,' I said. 'Thank you very much.'

She got this little push-chair out, and the baby came as good as gold – put its foot in the wheel a couple of times and nearly twisted its head off trying to see who I was, but I kept up the talking, and I stopped while it stared out a cat, so there wasn't any fuss.

When I got to the paper shop I took Bobby in with me.

'Afternoon,' I said, trying not to make too much of coming back. 'We've come for Mr Dawson's papers, haven't we, Bobby?'

You should have seen the man's face.

'Mr Dawson's?' he asked, burning his finger on a match. 'Number twenty-nine?'

'Yes, please.'

'Are you...?' He nodded at Bobby and then at me as if he was making some link between us.

'That's right,' I said.

He fumbled at a pile behind him and lifted out the magazines. He laid them on the counter.

'Dawson', it said on the top. I looked at the titles to see what Mr Dawson enjoyed reading.

Workers' Rights was one of them. And *Trade Union Times* was the other. They had pictures on their fronts. One had two men pulling together on a rope. The other had a woman bus-driver waving out of her little window. They told you the sort of man Mr Dawson was – one of those trade union people you get on television kicking up a fuss over wages, or getting cross when women are treated different to men. Just the sort of bloke I could do with on my side, I thought.

The man was still fiddling about with his pile of magazines.

'Oh, look,' he said, with a green grin. 'I've got last month's *Pop Today* left over. You can have it if you like, with my compliments...'

'Thanks a lot,' I said. Now I saw the link in his mind. He thought I was Mr Dawson's daughter. He thought there'd be all sorts of trouble now, over me being offered lower wages than the boys.

'And about that job. Stupid of me, I'd got it wrong. What did I say? *Four* pounds a week?'

'I think so,' I said. 'It sounded like a four.'

'How daft can you get? It was those kids in the corner. Took my attention off. Of course it's *five*, you realise that. Have you spoken to your dad yet?'

'No, not yet.'

He stopped leaning so hard on the counter. 'Are you still interested?'

'Yes. Thank you very much.'

He came round the front and shook hands with me. 'Monday at seven,' he said. 'Don't be late . . .' But you could tell he was only saying it, pretending to be the big boss.

'Right.' I turned the push-chair round. 'Say ta-ta to the man, Bobby,' I said.

Bobby just stared, like at the cat.

The paper-man leaned over. 'Dear little chap,' he said.

'Yeah, smashing. But Bobby's a girl, not a chap, aren't you, Bobby? At least, that's what Mrs Dawson just told me.'

I went out of the shop, while my new boss made this funny gurgling sound, and knocked a pile of papers on the floor.

He'd made a show-up of himself; found out too late that I wasn't Mr Dawson's daughter.

I ran and laughed and zigzagged Bobby along the pavement. 'Good for us! Equal rights, eh, Bobby? Equal rights!'

But Bobby's mind was all on the ride. She couldn't care less what I was shouting. All she wanted was someone to push her fast, to feel the wind on her face. Boy or girl, it was all the same to her.

Bernard Ashley

Questions to think and talk about

1   What do you think of the way the paper-man treated the girl at the beginning of the story?
2   Why did he change his mind? Does this change your opinion of him in any way?
3   The girl telling the story got her own way by means of a sort of trick. Was this fair?
4   If you had to sum up the character of the paper-man, what would you say?
5   How do you think he will treat the girl when she starts to work for him?

Reading aloud

This story contains two important conversations between the girl and the paper-man. They sound good if you read them aloud:

1   You need to work in a group of three or four:
      Paper-man
      Man with briefcase
      Girl
(If you have four, one person can read what the Girl says, and the other can read the story she is telling.)
2   Find the two conversations.
3   Work out who says what. For example, part of the first conversation goes like this:

GIRL: He frowned at me, in between watching the boys in the corner.
PAPER-MAN: What job?
GIRL: he said. He was all on edge . . .

4   Now practise your reading until you are satisfied with it.

Making a magazine

In this Special you are going to plan, design, write, and illustrate your own magazine pages. When you are planning and designing a magazine, there are three important things you need to think about.

Layout

This is the arrangement of words and pictures on the page. The layout should be interesting and lively, but also easy to understand.

Which of these layouts do you like best, and why?

Headings

Headings help the reader by showing what different parts of the page are about. They make it easier to find things. The style and size of headings are very important.

Which of these headings do you like, and why?

TALENT

Artwork

Most magazines make use of artwork:
    photographs (colour or black and white)
    line drawings
    charts
    diagrams
    full colour illustrations.
It is important to match the style of artwork to everything else on the page.
Which of these styles of illustration do you like best, and why?

Making a wall magazine page

You will need:
   a large sheet of paper
   smaller pieces of lined and plain paper
   rough paper
   pen
   pencil
   rubber
   coloured pencils or felt-tips
   scissors
   adhesive.

1   Decide on the theme for your page.
2   Decide the main items it will contain.
3   Make a rough plan of the layout.

4   Work out exactly how large each item should be to fit the layout.

5   If you are working in a group, decide who is doing what.
6   Write the articles.
7   Arrange the pieces of writing on the large sheet of paper, but **don't** stick them down yet.

8   Make illustrations and headings to fit the space that is left.

9   When everything is finished, stick all the pieces of paper onto the large sheet.

A whole magazine

Now you can go on to produce a whole magazine in the same way. Before you begin, you need to answer a number of questions.

- Who is your magazine going to be for?
- What will it contain?
- What will you call it?
- What will it look like?
- What materials do you need?
- What kind of pictures can you use?
- What is each page going to be about?
- Who is going to do what?

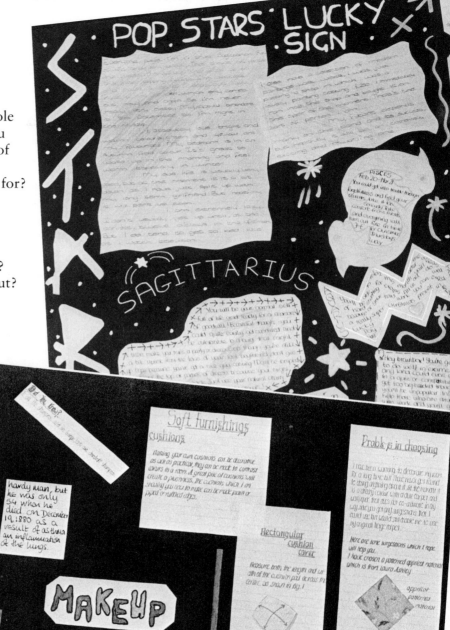

Past, present, future

1851

The Great Exhibition of the Works of Industry of All Nations was opened on 1 May 1851. It was a showpiece of the great strides made since the beginning of the Industrial Revolution. The building which housed the Exhibition was a great structure of glass and iron, 570 metres long and 125 metres wide, specially erected in Hyde Park in London. Inside the Crystal Palace, as it became known, the exhibits were arranged in four main sections, showing the latest examples of Raw Materials, Machinery, Manufactured Goods and The Arts. On display were such things as threshing-machines, model sawmills, model sailing-ships, power looms, steam-hammers, hydraulic jacks, locomotives and marine engines. There were 25,000 visitors on the first day alone.

Questions

Answer these questions for each of the exhibitions, 1851 and 1951.

1 In what city was it held?
2 How many different buildings are mentioned and what were they called?
3 What was the aim of the exhibition?
4 What were its main features?
5 What exhibits are mentioned?

2051?

Suppose another exhibition were to be held in 2051. What would it be like?

1951

The Festival of Britain was opened on 1 May 1951, to 'celebrate the beginning of a prosperous and enterprising future' after the hardships of two World Wars in the first half of the century. During the summer, eight million people visited the site on the south bank of the Thames. The Skylon, a thin cigar-shaped structure, towered above the site; the Dome of Discovery housed the wonders of science; the Festival Hall, which still stands, was built for special concerts and musical evenings; and Battersea Park became a huge pleasure-ground and fun-fair. Scientific discoveries, mechanical inventions and new materials (different kinds of plastics, steel furniture and man-made fabrics) illustrated Britain's continued progress.

Discussion

Think about the idea of holding such an exhibition in 2051.

1 Would it be a good idea, and, if so, why?
2 Where should it be held?
3 What do you think its aim might be?
4 What main features might it have?
5 What kinds of thing might be exhibited?

Writing

Write the story of 'How I visited the great exhibition of 2051.'

The Tay Bridge

The first Tay Bridge was opened on 31 May 1878. It was
designed by Sir Thomas Bouch and was hailed as a great
engineering achievement. At the time it was the longest
bridge over water in the world.

It was a girder bridge, a criss-cross of wrought iron girders   5
set on cast-iron columns on brick and concrete supports.
There were 85 spans (gaps between the supporting columns)
over two miles of the Firth of Tay, and the thirteen spans in
the middle of the river were wider than the rest, about 75
metres apart, to allow shipping to pass. The single track   10
railway, on the Edinburgh-Aberdeen line, ran between High
Girders in the central section of the bridge; otherwise there
were Low Girders below the level of the track towards each
bank.

In the early evening of Sunday, 28 December 1879, a   15
retired Admiral, who lived near the bridge, noted that a gale
force wind was blowing, with squalls which he estimated to
be 75–78 miles per hour. At 7o'clock the storm reached its
peak. At 7.20 a walnut tree in his garden was ripped out of
the ground.   20

At the bridge at 7.13, a mail train for Dundee slowed to
three miles per hour past the signal-box on the southern side.
In the box, John Watt and Thomas Bartlett watched the train
begin its journey across the bridge and disappear into the
darkness. At 7.20 they suddenly saw a flash in the blackness   25
of the night, and a streamer of light fell and vanished into the
dark waters of the Tay. The telegraph-lines were dead. The
two men crawled out along the track and found part of the
bridge gone. All thirteen High Girders and twelve cast-iron
supports had crashed into the river, taking with them the   30
whole train, with seventy-five men, women and children
aboard.

A Court of Enquiry was set up to investigate the accident, and the conclusion was that the Tay Bridge 'was badly designed, badly constructed and badly maintained, and its downfall was due to defects in the structure which must, sooner or later, have brought it down.' Some of the iron was badly cast, some of the joints were ill-fitting and cracks had already appeared in places and been patched up. One of the worst faults was that the design of the bridge made no allowance for wind pressure, although it was built in an area noted for its high winds.

Sir Thomas Bouch was held completely responsible for some of these defects, and partly responsible for others. He had had overall charge of the construction of the bridge, and he had to take the criticism. Within months of the enquiry he died, a broken man.

1   In which country was the Tay Bridge built? What clues are there in the passage to help you?
2   Why does the passage quote a retired Admiral giving his thoughts on the weather, rather than, say, a plumber or a baker?
3   Estimate in metres how much of the bridge collapsed.
4   For how long was the bridge in use?
5   What does a Court of Enquiry do? How is this done?
6   Explain: 'and its downfall . . . brought it down' (lines 36–8).
7   Was it fair to blame Sir Thomas Bouch for everything? Give your reasons.

8   Give another word, or words, for:
achievement (3)   estimated (17)
investigate (34)   defects (37)
ill-fitting (39)   held responsible (44)
overall charge (46) criticism (47)
9   Use the material in the passage as the basis for a short newspaper report of the collapse of the bridge.

Research

Find out what you can about the following examples of disastrous technology:
- The Ca 90 sea-plane (1921)
- The R 101 airship (1928)
- The Mariner I spacecraft (1962)
- The Chernobyl power station (1986).

Strange inventions

Which is the correct definition and why?

1a) An icebox
b) A coal bucket
c) A pressure-cooker
d) A camping-gas container

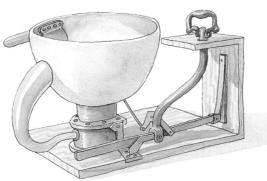

2a) A coffee-maker
b) A washing-machine
c) A food-mixer
d) A toilet

3a) A dog-harness
b) Headwear for rugby players
c) An instrument of torture
d) An anti-snoring device

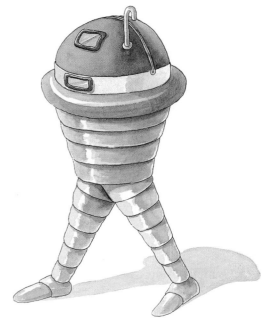

4a) An advertisement for tyres
b) A life-preserver at sea
c) A slimming-suit
d) Protection against poisonous gas

5a) A piano for beginners
b) A typewriter
c) A musical box
d) A fly-catcher

82

6 a) A clothes-drier
   b) A fan for hot climates
   c) A swimming machine
   d) An airborne bicycle

For each of these words, which is the correct definition?

7 The opera hat

a) was like a musical box. It was used to relieve boredom on long journeys. When the brim was twisted it would play a song from an opera; more expensive hats would play two or three.
b) was a hat worn at the opera. The hat was designed with a large hole in it so that the person behind could see the stage clearly.
c) was a hat worn to the opera. So that it could be stored neatly, the hat was designed to collapse into the brim.

8 The hackney

a) was a four-wheeled coach drawn by two horses. It could seat up to six people and was used for hire, like a modern taxi.
b) was a skin disease that affected teenagers especially. Various treatments reduced the unpleasant effects (see **The mangle**).
c) was a very small, or very young, robber, who took travellers by surprise. He would kick (**hacke**) his victim on the leg-joint, grab his purse, and make off with it.

9 The mangle

a) was a root vegetable, grown especially as winter food for cattle and sheep. When mashed (**mangled**) it was used as a paste to cure hackney.
b) was a device for squeezing water out of wet clothes. The clothes were passed between two rollers, which were rotated by a handle on the side of the machine.
c) was a fruit which was imported into Britain on board the early trading ships. Many people found the taste strange, but discovered that it made excellent chutney.

10 The post-horn

a) was used by wealthy people before the days of electric doorbells. Visitors would sound the horn, which hung beside the gate, to announce their arrival, and the host would be at the door to welcome them.
b) was a brass instrument, like a long trumpet, which was used on stage-coaches. It was blown to announce the arrival of the mail.
c) was a prickly plant which was discovered by Dr Walter Po (1736–1797) to be, in powdered form, a cure for the common cold. The plant has long been extinct.

What was it?

The grintern

Read these sentences and then follow the instructions.

a) 'Highly-polished, a selection of grinterns makes a charming decoration around this old stone fireplace.'
Felicity Grunge *Cottage and Mansion* October 1973

b) 'BY AUCTION: . . . and various old farm implements, including pitchforks, hay-rakes, shoe picks, grinterns, etc.'
Advertisement *Birmingham Evening Post* June 1932

c) 'Onions are best dried on grinterns, or anything else which allows the air to flow freely all around the vegetables.'
Allotment Holder's Magazine January 1910

d) '3 August 1807. John came in mid-morn with a nasty wounde from a grintern. How the bloode did poure! The doctor say he was lucky not to have lost an eye.'
Diary of Meg Morris (1787–1825)

e) 'Hanging baskets should be suspended in the greenhouse for two weeks for the plants to harden off. Grinterns are ideal for this purpose.'
J. Smedley *Gardening for Beginners* 1886, reprinted 1959

Instructions

1 Explain what a grintern is.
2 Explain what it is made of, and what it is used for.
3 If necessary, use a drawing to help your explanation.

The posser

Now do the same for a **posser**.

a) 'The contrasting materials of something as common as a posser can be very effective in emphasising light and shade.'
Dennis Baily *Indoor Photography* 1937

b) 'As the electric washing-machine becomes more and more popular, things like the posser will soon be forgotten.'
Talk on *BBC Radio* December 1948

c) 'The noise was unrelenting. He knew he could not take much more. On and on it went. He felt like a shirt being pounded by a posser on a Monday morning.'
Marvin Q. Megler *A Pretty Way to Die?* 1940

d) 'For this you need two possers. Take out the broom handle things, and tape the copper bits together . . . See? A lovely shiny ball. Now, I'll just put some holly and bits of Christmas tree in the holes . . . some more sticky-back plastic . . . And some strong wire in here to hang it up with . . . There, a lovely decoration for your home this Christmas.'
Children's TV programme December 1966

The past-present-future table

Study the table opposite. What do you think should go in the spaces with question marks?

1 Write down what you think should go in each space.
2 Explain why you think so.

PAST	PRESENT	FUTURE
		?
?		?
		?
	?	?
	?	?
?		?

When I was your age . . .

Anyone under 21 should not be allowed near a football ground. They are all hooligans – out looking for trouble.

People over 70 aren't fit to drive cars. They shouldn't be allowed on the road. They're a menace!

The pop music industry takes teenagers for a ride. Look at all the money they spend. Put a pop star's name on something and it costs the earth!

If you have an opinion, you must be prepared to give people your reasons.

1   Look at each statement in turn.
2   Do you agree or disagree?

3   Write **one sentence** for each statement, saying **why** you agree or disagree.

Building up the argument

Choose at least one of these statements about young people. Give your views on it. Write at least three or four sentences.

Too cheeky by half, that young man. He's like the rest of them – far too much to say for himself.

Children today don't know what manners are!

Work? Youngsters are frightened of it nowadays!

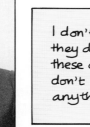

I don't know what they do at school these days. They don't seem to learn anything.

Looking at both sides

The arguments below are in pairs.

1   Choose one of the pairs.
2   Divide a page in your exercise book into two columns.
3   In one column write all the arguments you can think of on the side of **A**.
4   In the other column do the same for **B**.
5   At the bottom of the page write down what **you** think.

A. Fox-hunting is totally unnecessary. There's no excuse for it — it's cruel.

B. It's natural for foxes to be chased, and it keeps down pests.

A. Animal experiments are senseless cruelty to defenceless creatures.

B. Well, it's a bit sad, but it's better than experimenting on people.

A. I don't want to do homework when I've been at school all day — it's pointless.

B. Homework makes you listen in class and proves you can work on your own.

Remembering

'Mr Treloar,' said Nancy, 'Frances would like to interview you.'

'Interview?' he said, jerking his head up and drawing his brows together so that the two deep lines appeared in his forehead.

'It's her work for school,' said Nancy. 'She'd like to ask you some questions.'

'What does she want to know?'

'She wants to know about you.'

'About me?' He looked across at his wife, whose eyes were closed, her head nodding. 'Why does she want to know about me

'Because you've lived a long life and you've seen a lot of changes.'

'I have,' he agreed.

'You tell Fran about them, while I go and see another patient.' She got up to go. 'I'll come back and pick you up in about an hour,' she said to Fran.

'But . . . I thought you were going to stay.'

'I'm supposed to be working.'

'I thought you'd put the questions; he never understands me.'

'Go on, you'll be all right!' said Nancy. 'Speak into his left ear, like I do . . . I'll see you later.'

She was gone, and the only sounds in the room were the drawn-in breaths of Mr Treloar, the gentle snoring of his wife, and the ticking of the grandfather clock in the hall. The wind sighed in the trees above the farm.

Fran returned the drawer of mineral specimens to the dresser, and sat on the chair. She leaned towards the old man, closer than she would normally speak to anyone; she felt uneasy and a little repelled by the closeness. She could smell his body and his clothes. It was not unpleasant, nor pleasant neither; a sort of soapy smell, with a slight sourness underneath it.

'Mr Treloar,' she said, 'where were you born?'

'Eh?' he asked. He had turned the side of his face towards her, and now darted his head round to look at her.

She wished her mother had been there as interpreter. She tried to imitate her way of emphasising the last word.

'Where were you **born**?'

To her relief, he understood. 'I was born in this house.'

'How long ago?'

'Eighty-nine years ago; I shall be ninety next birthday,' he said. 'My father was a tenant farmer, just as his father before him. And then when I was a boy the squire had to sell some of his property, and my father bought the farm.'

Fran scribbled down as much as she could in the notebook on

her lap. Once he had started, Mr Treloar did not need much prompting. He described how he left school at fourteen, to start work on the farm. The boys with father and brothers who were miners left at an earlier age, to go into the mines. A farm-lad was paid five shillings a week, and worked from seven to five, six days a week and every other Sunday morning.

He turned towards the dresser. 'Open that long drawer!' he ordered. In the middle drawer of the dresser she found what he was looking for, several photograph albums. They had padded brown covers, and were held together with faded gold braid. She opened one; the pages were interleaved with tissue paper which had a spider's web design, and through the web the fading brown photographs showed dimly. She turned over the tissue. The photos recorded the life of the farm, and he spoke as though it was all still fresh in his mind. He pointed out a brown photograph labelled in white ink, 'Croust at haymaking'. It showed a large hay-mow with a party of workers sitting beneath it, the men in shirt sleeves and the women in sun-bonnets. The sun shone into their eyes, and they squinted at the camera. In front of them were baskets and ewers.

'What's croust?' Fran asked.

'Croust?' he questioned. 'Why, it's the food a miner takes down the mine, or a farmer eats in the fields. Our croust was always a saffron bun about the size of a dinner plate, and hot, milky coffee.'

He passed the album to his wife, who woke up.

'That's at Trengoose,' she said.

'Of course it's not!' he shouted. 'It's at Penhallow!'

'Oh yes,' she said.

Fran looked at photos of threshing-machines and traction-engines, horses and cows, the farm under snow.

'That was the shooting house,' he said, pointing to a building with long icicles hanging from the roof.

Fran thought it was a sort of slaughterhouse. 'What did you shoot?' she asked.

He laughed, very pleased with her slightly shocked reaction.

'It's where we put the potatoes to sprout – the shooting house!'

She glanced up at him, and saw that he had said it to tease her. She smiled at the old-fashioned joke.

John Branfield *Fox in Winter*

Croust at Haymaking.

What do you think Fran wrote in her notebook? Read the story carefully and then write what she put down.

Time capsule

2089

Leicester
21 October 1989

To whoever discovers this box

We are a group of children living towards the end of the twentieth century. We have decided to bury some typical objects from our time. If anything happens to our world, we hope these objects will show you what our society was like - how it was different from yours and how it was similar. We have included some extra notes to describe our way of life.

Goodbye.

1989

What shall we tell them about?

Dangers Home Pastimes Science Technology Education

What to do

1   Make a list of things to include in the box. They must be typical of life today. They mustn't be too big – the box is only 1 metre × 1 metre × 1 metre. You could include books, plans, paper, etc.
2   Choose the **six** best objects from your list.
3   Write a brief description of each one, and explain why you have chosen it.
4   Write a page describing life today.

This is what was put in the box...

Diaries and letters

1988

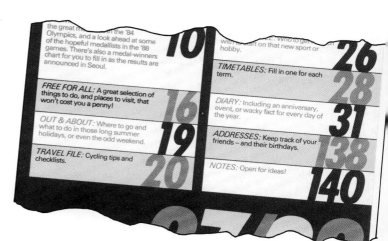

the great m...in the '84 Olympics, and a look ahead at some of the hopeful medallists in the '88 games. There's also a medal-winners chart for you to fill in as the results are announced in Seoul.

FREE FOR ALL: A great selection of things to do, and places to visit, that won't cost you a penny!

OUT & ABOUT: Where to go and what to do in those long summer holidays, or even the odd weekend.

TRAVEL FILE: Cycling tips and checklists.

10

...with to start on that new sport or hobby.

TIMETABLES: Fill in one for each term.

DIARY: Including an anniversary, event, or wacky fact for every day of the year.

ADDRESSES: Keep track of your friends – and their birthdays.

NOTES: Open for ideas!

26 28 31 138 140

16 19 20

1988 **DIARY**

Collins

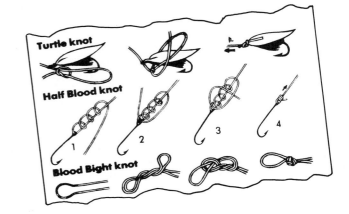

Turtle knot

Half Blood knot 1 2 3 4

Blood Bight knot

BREAKFAST THATCH

This savoury breakfast recipe was sent to us by Mrs Gladys Flinders of Quorn, N... Loughborough. "Children will love this unusual breakfast recipe. I... send them to school on, especially on chill...

5
Monday Week 41 PAYE week 27

6
Tuesday

7
Wednesday

Questions

1 What do you think is the title of each of the diaries on the facing page?
2 What kind of person would be likely to buy each of these diaries?
3 What sort of special information would you expect each one to contain?

Writing

1 Choose one of the diaries and make a detailed list of the information and illustrations you would expect to find in it.

2 Although there are many specialist diaries, there may not be one for a particular interest of yours. Name a specialist diary you would like to see, and make a list of what it should contain.

Extra-specialist diaries

Have you ever thought what an extra-specialist diary would look like?

Writing

1 Choose one of the diaries.
2 Fill in the spaces, as if it was **your** diary.
3 Make a list of other specialist information you think this diary should contain.

Keeping a diary

SUNDAY 31 JANUARY

Tried to do Eng. homework
Can't find book.
HATE SUNDAYS!

MONDAY 1 FEBRUARY

Mike's party - DISASTROUS!
no records tape machine broken,
not enough food fizz or
fellers. Left v. early.

TUESDAY 2 FEBRUARY

Another bad day. V. wet.
Borrowed Di's coat. Left it
on bus. What shall I do?
X BAD DAY

WEDNESDAY 3 FEBRUARY

Rang L.T. depot. No news of coat.
Haven't told Di. Saw P.R. today
GREAT!! ♥ ×××××××

THURSDAY 4 FEBRUARY

Hempley Disco with Chrissie and
Okker! WOW! Most groups 11/10
The Warthogs 1200/10 But the
Greeboes -1/10. P.R. there
(SWOON!) ♥ ×××××

FRIDAY 5 FEBRUARY

Saw Mike. P.R. is going out with
Anna. He's a CREEP anyway.
No news of coat still haven't
told Di   UGH!

SATURDAY 6 FEBRUARY

Great! LT have found coat!
p.m. SPURS v FOREST.
USELESS - HT: 0-1 FT: 1-3

Questions

1 This diary uses a lot of abbreviations.
  What do you think each of these means?

Eng	P.R.
v.	HT
Di	FT
LT	

2 There are two 'stories' in this diary:
   a) about the mac
   b) about P.R.
   What happens in each one?

3 What kind of person is keeping this
  diary? What makes you think this?

4 Tell the story of the week, day by day,
  writing out what happened, using
  complete words and complete sentences.

Most people have written diaries at some time. Often they look back at them and wonder why they bothered. The main reason for this is that people tend to do the same things day after day. Their lives are **routine**. This doesn't mean that they or their lives are boring. Firemen, shepherds and brain surgeons live lives that are routine to them – but they wouldn't be to you. If you read their diaries you would probably find them interesting – but only if they were well written. In the same way, your diary might be very interesting to them.

Writing a diary

Keep your own diary for a week. Write it at the end of each day when events are still fresh in your mind. Try to make it interesting for you to read afterwards. Here are some suggestions for things you could include:

1   People you talked to, and what you talked about.
2   Things that happened at home.
3   Things that made you angry, or amused, or sad, or . . .
4   Things you read, or saw on TV, that were special or interesting.
5   Anything in the day's news that interested you.
6   Important things that you have been thinking about.

Writing about your week

At the end of the week, read through what you have written. Select the most interesting bits and use them to write an account of **A week in my life**.

How to set out a letter

A letter should include:

① Your full address.

② The date.

③ The greeting:
Dear Jane if you know the person well.
Dear Ms/Mrs/Miss/Mr if you have met them, but do not know them well.
Dear Madam/Sir if you have never met them, or don't know their name.

④ The letter.

⑤

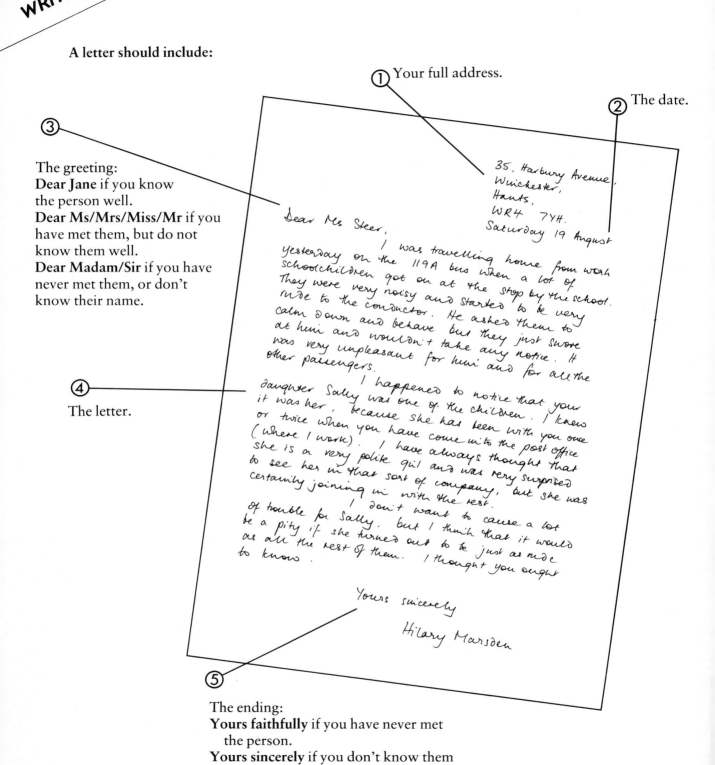

35, Harbury Avenue,
Winchester,
Hants,
WR4 7YH.
Saturday 19 August

Dear Mrs Steer,
          I was travelling home from work yesterday on the 119A bus when a lot of schoolchildren got on at the stop by the school. They were very noisy and started to be very rude to the conductor. He asked them to calm down and behave but they just swore at him and wouldn't take any notice. It was very unpleasant for him and for all the other passengers.
          I happened to notice that your daughter Sally was one of the children. I knew it was her, because she has been with you once or twice when you have come into the post office (where I work). I have always thought that she is a very polite girl and was very surprised to see her in that sort of company, but she was certainly joining in with the rest.
          I don't want to cause a lot of trouble for Sally, but I think that it would be a pity if she turned out to be just as rude as all the rest of them. I thought you ought to know.

                    Yours sincerely
                    Hilary Marsden

The ending:
Yours faithfully if you have never met the person.
Yours sincerely if you don't know them very well.
Use a more informal ending if you know them well, for example **Best wishes.**

When you are addressing an envelope, include:

① The title (Ms, Miss, Mrs, Mr).

② The initials and name of the person.

③ The number of the house and the street.

④ The town.

⑤ The county.

⑥ The post-code.

Ms S. Steer,
39, Grangemouth Road,
Angleton,
Clwyd,
CF4 6FS

Writing a reply

Imagine that you are Ms Steer. How would you reply to Mrs Marsden's letter?

1 Decide how you would feel about what she says. What would you say to your daughter? How might she reply?
2 Decide on the main things you would say in reply to Mrs Marsden.
3 Now write the letter. Make sure that you set it out correctly.

4 Draw a rectangle to be the 'envelope'. Address it correctly to Mrs Marsden.

Absence note

You are the parent of the girl in this story. Write a letter to the headteacher of your school explaining why she has been absent.

Diary or letter?

Dear Auntie Mabel,
          Thank you for having me for the weekend. I always look forward to coming to see you.

Monday
Got back late from Auntie M's. Thank goodness that's over for another year. Boring, boring, boring!

We do not like to hurt some people, but in a diary we can express our true feelings.
This is how the letter and diary went on.

Writing

Write out the letter and the diary in full, filling in the spaces with suitable words or phrases.

The afternoon out to see cousin Colin was a great .... All those budgerigars! He must find it very .... I should think he's ....
...., waiting for the eggs to hatch and watching the little ones grow.

The .... of the weekend had to be the .... Village Concert. What a ....! I was .... by the extraordinary ....
.... of talent. How do they do it? The vicar's singing was ....,
and Auntie Vi's ventriloquist act was .... I've seen nothing like it! The dancers were all ....,
and so .... with it; and little Joanne's acrobatics were ....
All in all, it was by far the ....
show I have seen ....

On Saturday afternoon we went to see cousin Colin and his ....
budgerigars! What a ....!
He must find it .... I think he's ...., just sitting around waiting for the eggs to hatch.

The .... of the weekend was the .... Village Concert.
What a ....! I was .... by the extraordinary .... of talent. Why do they do it? The vicar's singing was ...., and Auntie Vi's ventriloquist act was .... I've seen nothing like it!
The dancers were all ...., and so .... with it; and little Joanne's acrobatics were ....
All in all ....

Writing

Look at the story above. Following the pattern on page 96, write a **thank you** letter and a diary entry about this story.

or Something like this might have happened to you, or perhaps you can think of a different situation. Write the letter and diary entry for your own story.

Dear Emily

2 February.

Dear Emily,

You don't know me. I have chosen you to be my pen-friend. Our English teacher said it would be a good thing if we all chose a pen-friend, as it would help with our writing. I chose you from a list of people wanting pen-friends in last Sunday's paper. I hope you haven't had so many letters that you can't reply to me.

I chose you for two reasons. I like the sound of your name, and you live in the country. I've only been to the country once (so I'm told, I was only one at the time).

I'll tell you a bit about myself. I am an intensely interesting person. I've worked hard at being interesting, because I'm not much to look at. I blame that on my father, who is one of the least impressive human beings you would ever see. My name – would you believe – is Maria. I hate it. There are five Marias in our class. I am by far the most exciting of the five.

I live in Richmond, in Melbourne, with my glamorous mother and scruffy father, and a brother who is best ignored. I go to South Richmond High, and I'm fourteen, just.

My mother is an executive with a cosmetics company (actually she sells Avon stuff door to door, but what I said sounds more impressive, if you know what I mean). My father is a public servant and does nothing.

I could tell you more about myself and my family but it has just occurred to me that would be a waste of time, as you mightn't answer this letter.

I bet you are the only one called Emily in your class. Please answer soon and tell me about yourself and your family and everything.

Your pen-friend (I hope!)
Maria Smales

17 February.

Dear Emily,
Thank you for your letter! I am so glad you will be my pen-friend. I will answer your questions first.
1 No, I don't have braces on my teeth. Mind you, I probably should have, as they are a bit much – I mean, too much of them, and they stick out a bit when I smile, but with my life-style I don't get to smile much so I suppose it doesn't matter all that much.
2 My hair is brown and my eyes are blue.
3 Yes, I get pimples, and there is a simple reason for this. For some time now my mother has been a vegetarian and a health food freak and so I don't get to eat normal things like chips and pies and soft drinks, so my skin suffers terribly, and so does my stomach.
4 I don't share your love of magazines! I think they are trashy. The ones my mother reads are all about clothes and make-up and diets and I was bored by them by the time I was ten. She might be glamorous but her mind is pretty slight.
5 No, it is not a contradiction to say that my father is in the public service and does nothing. I suppose you don't have public servants in the country, so you wouldn't know about them. Actually he is a clerk in the railways but I prefer to call him a public servant. It makes him sound more intelligent than he really is.
6 I can't answer questions about my brother, because he is really best ignored, as I mentioned in my first letter.
7 No, I suppose I didn't sound intensely interesting in my letter, but you see, Emily, I didn't know if you would reply, and so I didn't tell you much about myself in case I was wasting time. But

now that I know I'm not, here is more information about me. I hate all herb teas and I detest mushrooms, egg-plant, zucchini, and anything made from soya beans. Soya beans taste like mud. Most food my mother cooks contains some of the above detested foods. Are there any vegetarians in the country? I suppose not, because you eat cows and sheep and things there. Do you have any cows or sheep? You said your father was a farmer. That must be wonderful. Does he wear jeans and a cowboy hat? My father wears grey suits and it matches his grey job and grey personality. He sort of melts into the footpath.

I think I began to be interesting when I was about four. That's when I saw through fairy tales and bible stories.

8 No, I don't know what I want to be when I finish school. I might write television scripts, or work in a pet shop. Why do you want to be a cabinet-maker? Why don't you try for some job outside in the fresh air, like maybe the person who holds the flag for road-workers? I've thought of that one myself.

I'd better close now, because I've got some maths homework. You are so lucky to have a cat and two dogs. We live in a flat and can't have animals. It must be wonderful to live in the country. What do you have for breakfast?

Your pen-friend,
Maria

PS No, I didn't get any Valentine cards. I think they are silly and fit for tiny minds like my mother's. She got three.

1 March.

Dear Emily,
I didn't mean you had a tiny mind!

You mustn't take things so personally. And I wasn't rude about the magazines you like. I just don't like them myself. Did I really say they were trashy? I forget, but, if I did, I'm sorry. I mean, they are of course, but I shouldn't have said so. Some people get so easily hurt. I am not one of those people, I can take anything.

I can't believe you haven't heard of soya beans or egg-plant. You are so **lucky!** And I'd give anything to have bacon and eggs most mornings for breakfast. We have home-made muesli and I won't tell you what it looks like. It tastes like it too.

What I meant by my father melting into the footpath was not that he gets fainting attacks. I don't know if you have ever been to Melbourne, but the footpaths are grey, and so in his grey clothes he sort of looks like part of the footpath. Do you have footpaths in the country?

And, Emily, I wasn't trying to be smart about seeing through fairy stories and bible stories. I **am** smart. I don't try to be. How was I supposed to know you were a Christian? Live and let live, I say, but you wouldn't. You'd say 'an eye for an eye and a tooth for a tooth', wouldn't you? I suppose your parents made you believe in the tooth fairy and Santa Claus, too. At least even my dad didn't try any of that with me. You believe what you like, and I'll do likewise.

But what do you mean when you write that 'it's nice for children to believe in fairy stories'? **Nice?** To believe in talking wolves that eat grandmothers? And wicked stepmothers who try to poison their stepdaughters? I mean, did you **really** believe in Little Red Riding Hood and Snow White? Do people in the country all believe in things like that?

What are your dogs called? What's your school like?

Your friend,
Maria

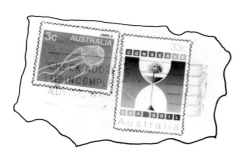

19 March.

Dear Emily,
Thanks for your letter, and the photos of your dogs. I like their names. I mean, calling the black one Blackie and the white one Snow shows a sort of imagination, don't you think?

Your school sounds terrific. All that grass, and trees! Our playground (it's called that, believe it or not, even though it's a high school) is all cement.

Thanks for your photo. You look really cute in your uniform. Are long skirts coming back into fashion? I'll get one of myself for you. Is that your mum with you in the photo, or your grandmother? She looks nice, anyway. Wait till you see a photo of my mum – she looks like a model. Unfortunately, I didn't inherit her looks, but fortunately I didn't inherit her brain either.

Emily, I didn't say that country people were stupid. How could I say that when you are the only one I know? And I never generalise. And I certainly didn't say you probably believed in the tooth fairy. I meant you probably did **years** ago, when your baby teeth were falling out. And so what if you did? You made some money out of it.

Here's the Avon catalogue you asked for. I wouldn't buy any if I were you. I suppose you don't have Avon ladies in the country because it's too far to walk between farms. Mum said to thank your mother for her pumpkin scone recipe. She is going to make some tomorrow, when she has her Assertiveness Group. Does your mum go to those too?

No, my father doesn't go to Rotary meetings. I asked him why not, and he said they were for small men who toasted the Queen. My father's tall, and he wouldn't hurt a fly, so I guess he wouldn't fit in at a Rotary meeting.

Your boy-friend sounds interesting. No, I don't have one at the moment. As I've mentioned, Emily, I don't look attractive or anything, and I don't think boys like interesting girls anyway. They like them pretty and dumb, and I'm neither of those!

Anyway, that's all for now. Since you asked, my brother's name is Gregory Francis Smales, and he's sixteen and, no, he hasn't a girl-friend. Who'd have him?

If you really want to get some Avon stuff, the violet cream perfume is okay.

Your friend,
Maria

Maureen Stewart   *Dear Emily*

Questions to think about

1   This extract consists of four letters from Maria to Emily. In between them Emily wrote back:

Maria to Emily   **Emily to Maria**

a) 2 February

                                           b) _____

c) 17 February

                                           d) _____

e) 1 March

                                           f) _____

g) 19 March

We haven't got letters b), d) and f), but we can work out what they must have said, from what Maria writes next. What do you think they said?

2   What kind of person do you think Maria is? What are your reasons?

Writing

Write one of Emily's letters – b), d) or f).

104

Famous diaries

On the next three pages are extracts from four
famous diaries. There are also descriptions
and pictures of famous people who wrote
diaries. Who wrote which extract?

A Wednesday 8th July.
A bit later, Margot appeared at the kitchen door looking very
excited. 'The SS have sent a call-up notice for Daddy,' she
whispered. 'Mummy has gone to see Mr Van Daan already.' It was
a great shock to me, a call-up; everyone knows what that means. I
picture concentration camps and lonely cells – should we allow
him to be doomed to this? 'Of course he won't go,' declared
Margot, while we waited together. 'Mummy has gone to the Van
Daans to discuss whether we should move into our hiding-place
tomorrow. The Van Daans are going with us, so we shall be seven
in all.' Silence . . . Into hiding – where would we go, in a town or
the country, in a house or a cottage, when, how, where?

   Margot and I began to pack some of our most vital belongings
into a school satchel. The first thing I put in was this diary.

B March ye 11. – Tomorrow bein Lords day Sarah and me to
making pies for dinner, and to cleaning up the kitchens and
passages.

   In comes Mistress Prue at midday to tell me Joe Shorts wiffe do
have a child and she with littel clothes for it, bein verrie poor. So I
with Mistress Prue to see the poor wretch, and did find her lying
most worrie and comfurtless.

   I back home to get some clean sheets and a blankit to make the
poor sowl better, and some milk for her to drink; which did warm
her.

   I did not tell John of me giving her the sheets and blankit, he
bein a mere man so it not wise to do so. Yet I could but think how
much better off I be to hav a good bed to lie on, and plenty of
vittels to my inside. I should not like to live in a hovel like Emma
Short.

C **2nd (Lord's day).** Some of our maids sitting up late last night to get things ready against our feast today, Jane called us up about three in the morning, to tell us of a great fire they saw in the City. So I rose, and slipped on my night-gown, and went to her window; and thought it to be on the back-side of Marke-lane at the farthest, but being unused to such fires as followed, I thought it far enough off; and so went to bed again, and to sleep. About seven rose again to dress myself, and there looked out of the window, and saw the fire not so much as it was, and further off. By and by Jane comes and tells me that she hears that above 300 houses have been burned down to-night by the fire we saw, and that it is now burning down all Fish-street, by London Bridge.

1

2

3

The writers

Edith B. Holden lived in Warwickshire, and worked as an illustrator of books. Her paintings of plants, birds and animals bring colour to her book, which is called *The Country Diary of an Edwardian Lady*.

Anne Frank was a young girl of a Jewish family, who kept a diary for two years when the German army occupied Holland in the early 1940s. Most of the diary was written when she, her family and some friends were in hiding.

The diary of **Anne Hughes** was first published in the 1930s. It is supposed to have been written in 1796–7, by the wife of a farmer living in Herefordshire. People now believe that this diary is not genuine, but is a twentieth-century fake.

Samuel Pepys lived in the 17th century, and kept his diary for nine years. He lived in London and knew many famous people of the time. He also recorded a number of important historical events.

D Friday 16 March or Saturday 17.

Lost track of dates, but think the last correct. Tragedy all along the line. At lunch, the day before yesterday, poor Titus Oates said he couldn't go on; he proposed we should leave him in his sleeping-bag. That we couldn't do, and we induced him to come on, on the afternoon march. In spite of its awful nature for him he struggled on and we made a few miles. At night he was worse and we knew the end had come.

He has borne intense suffering for weeks without complaint. He was a brave soul. This was the end. He slept through the night before last, hoping not to wake; but he woke in the morning – yesterday. It was blowing a blizzard. He said, 'I am just going outside and may be some time.' He went out into the blizzard and we have not seen him since.

4

Adrian Mole is a fictional character created by Sue Townsend. His diary tells of the worries of a modern teenager as he records the day-to-day life of those around him.

Captain Robert Falcon Scott was a British explorer who died in 1912 when returning to base camp from an expedition to the South Pole. His diary tells of hardship, quiet courage and outstanding heroism.

Questions

On the left there are pictures which show four of the writers described below. Which is which and which two are not illustrated?

For each diary extract, answer these questions:

1   What kind of person do you think s/he was?
2   What impression do you get of life at the time the diary was written?
3   What do you think of the way in which the diary is written?

Writing

One of these extracts is written in dialect, that is, the way people speak in a particular community. Choose **one** of the entries in your own diary (page 95), and rewrite it in your own dialect, or in one which is very familiar to you.

School trip

The competition

There is a competition to plan the best school trip. There are four things you have to do:

1   make the **plan,**
2   book the **coach,**
3   make up the **information sheet,**
4   work out the **timetable.**

The plan

1   **Where?**
      Where would you like to go?
        zoo
        pleasure park
        seaside
        castle or other historic place
        more than one place
2   **Why?**
      What are the advantages of going to the place(s) you have chosen?
3   **How far?**
      Some people don't like long coach journeys. How far is the place that you have chosen?
4   **Who?**
        All of your year group
        Just your class
        Your class and another class
5   **How many coaches?**
      You can get 35-, 45- or 52-seater coaches. What will you need?
6   **How many teachers?**
      If there are boys and girls going, you need one male teacher and one female teacher for each coach. So how many do you need?
      Without naming names, what kind of teachers do you need?

Think about all these things and then write out your plan.

The information sheet

Each pupil will need an information sheet to take home. This will tell the people at home what has been planned. Think about the things they will want to know. These will include the information you gave the coach company. Then there is:

- How much it will cost.
- What food and drink the children need to take.
- What special clothing they should take.
- How much pocket-money they will need.
- The main things that they will see and do.

Think about these things. Then make up your information sheet.

The timetable

Everyone will need to know the details of
the day's events. You might have a strict
timetable, or just a list of things that people
can do at different times if they want to. Your
timetable depends on:

- Whether everyone is going to stay together
  all the time.
- Whether children will go round in groups
  with a teacher.
- Whether they will go round on their own.
  (If so, how do they find a teacher if they
  need to?)
- Whether they will all meet up at any time,
  for example, at dinner time.
- Whether there is anything that you will
  have to book the group in for (like a film).

Think about all these things and then make
up a timetable for the day.

The coach

You are going to write a letter to the coach
company, to book the coach(es) you will
need. They will need some details:

- Date of the trip.
- Time of departure.
- Time you want to get back.
- Number of children.
- Number of teachers.

You will need some information, particularly
how much it will cost.

Work out what you want to say.
If you are not sure how to set the letter out,
look at page 96. Now write your letter.

What happens on the trip?

First impressions

What is the scene around you like?
What is the weather like?
What do you hear, see, smell?
Do you get the feeling that this is going to be a good day?
Describe in detail the first things that strike you about the place you are visiting, and describe your feelings.

Something's happened!

'It's Diane, Mr Leason.'
'What about her?'
'She was just going to . . . . , and then –'
'What happened?'
'I don't really know, but now she's . . . .'
Something has happened!
What is it?
   An accident?
   Someone missing?
   Something funny?

It may have happened to Diane, or to anyone in your class. Decide what has happened, work out what happens in the end, and then tell the story.

Now what?

During the day all sorts of interesting, amusing and strange things happen to people in your class. You are going to tell the story of one of them. It involves four of the people or things shown in the picture. Choose four and then make up a story which includes all four. Describe it as though it was happening to you.

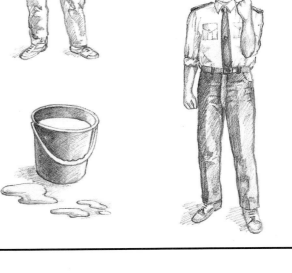

Time to go

'Well, we can't wait for them much longer.'
'We can't just go and leave them here.'
'So what are we going to do?'
Continue the story. Some things you could think about:

- What will happen to the rest of the party if there is a long delay?
- What will happen to the missing children if they are left behind?
- Why have they not kept to the timetable?
- What do the two teachers think about these children normally (in school)?
- What happens in the end?

Think about all these things, then write the story of what happens.

Drafting : The memory poem

Drafting means writing something more than once, in order to
develop and improve your ideas. You write, correct, and rewrite
until you are satisfied. These four pages show how three people in
the same class wrote a memory poem.

Stage 1: a starting point

112

Stage 2 : getting some ideas down

Now I want you to write whatever comes into your head about that memory. It doesn't matter if you start writing about something else. Just write quickly.

The running track

Tree

Humanities Hut
French wine posters
Double doors *

Sports day I am at the start ready to go Mr turner ~~says~~ raises the gun "on your marks" "get set" Bang! the gun fires and we race away I ~~had~~ put a~~t~~ lot of effort into the start and get away well we ~~run as are all putting all or~~ race with all our strength~~s~~ 25 metres ~~all our streng~~ I am winning~~s~~ but I must go faster 50 meters my legs pump away like the pistons of a train but in the corner of my eye I see Brendon. ~~I can not beat him~~ 75 meters I can not win Brendon is to far ahead on the line ~~I can lose~~ 95 meters and another boy passes me 100 meters and I cross the line 3rd.

What Ian wrote.

What Becky wrote.

Across the way where I used to live was a great big field full of poppys and old blocks of concrete e I ~~too~~ tree. We had just moved into the house which was brand new. It was in Watford. Me e my friend drew pictures on the concrete blocks with the black bits of the poppys. Or we had sword fights with bamboo canes once I had to go to the doctors because of this fight. I had cut myself really deeply and I had to have butterfly stitches and a big bandage on my finger. We didn't have a road in front of our house but just had a path. The path was new tarmac and you could dig it up e make pictures when the weather was warm. It was all black e ▓▓▓▓ gungy and smelt really funny. Big ▓▓▓ rollers would come down the road to flatten the path. There were bits of houses still being built down our road.

What Nick wrote.

Eye operation November two years ago in Bristol Homeopathic Hospital. Went in on a Teusday and got used to bed, people, food Not ~~allowed~~ to eat after lunch, hungry all night. Wednesday morning given injection to make me feel drowsy then put on to a metal bed and wheeled away through several pairs of double doors which ~~swing~~ when I was pushed through ~~them~~ came to a stop once in a large white walled room ~~with two doctors and three~~ ~~nurses in it.~~ They told me to squeeze my hand into a fist and back again while ~~a band~~ was put round my arm. Then a ~~needle~~ was put into a vein on the ~~back~~ of my hand and was asleep in about a minute. When I woke up, it was ~~thurs~~ Wednesday night and had to go to sleep again. I was awake most of the night because ~~I was either sick~~ the kid next to me was screaming because he didn't want to go the OR Thursday morning my Mum & Dad came to see me and brought me a bottle of Lucozade, a bar of chocolate and a bunch of very sour grapes. was sick on the Lucozade and couldn't eat the grapes. The chocolate bar didn't last long though.

Our house was new, we'd just moved in
Me my mum & dad and baby sister
And Blue the dog.
I played with my friend who lived down
the road
With concrete blocks and long bamboo canes
And ground down poppy pestals
We painted pictures on the blocks of stone
That were in the poppy fields across the path.
And drew in the new black tarmac
I had a small red tricycle which I rode
Or I scrambled in the knee high grass
And I often went home with a scraped knee
or a dress torn or finger cut
Down the hill were half built houses
a place forbidden for me to play
and scaffolding and bricks were scattered
across the path
and into the fields beyond.
across the path & the fields.

Becky

Now you've got another ten minutes. Start organising what you've written into a poem. Concentrate on what you really want to say. Try to add some extra details. Make sure that you've chosen exactly the right words. Cut out anything that isn't really important.

Once I had an eye operation one November
I went in on a Tuesday getting used
to food, people, bed, food,
Hungry all night.
Wednesday morning and needle time, sleepy time
wheeled away to a large white walled room
Needle again, sleepy again.
Sleep.
Woke on Thursday.
Food from mum and dad.
Lucozade, grapes sour grapes, chocolate

Lucozade remains
Sour grapes remain
Chocolate ?
Home on Thursday.

_____

I awoke on Thursday
Food from Mum & Dad
Lucozade still undrunk
Sourgrapes still uneaten
Chocolate?
Home on Thursday.

Nick

It is Sports day

I am ready for the start of my
race The Starter raises his pistol
" On your marks "
I crouch down
"Set "
I redy myself
Bang
I go
I grin
A lot of efort at the Start
I am winning
25 metres
My legs pump away like pistons
50 metres now
I see Brendon
75 metres
I cannot win anymore
Brendon to far ahead
95 metres
Another boy passes me
Here's the line
Third.

Ian

Seeing how it works

1 Choose one of the three writers: Nick, Becky, or Ian.
2 Follow your writer's poem through the four stages.
3 Notice the changes that happen at each stage.
4 Can you see why the writer made those changes?

Stage 4 : polishing

This time you can take as long as you like. Divide your writing up into lines, so that when you read it, it sounds right. Look again at the words you have chosen. — are they right for the job? Does the poem say exactly what you want it to?

Becky's poem.

Our house was new, we'd just moved in
Me my mum and dad and baby sister
And 'Blue' the dog
I played with my friend who lived down
the road

With concrete blocks & long bamboo canes
And red poppy petals
We painted pictures on the blocks of
stone

That were in the poppy fields across the path
And drew in the new black tarmac
I had a small red tricycle which I rode
Or scrambled in the kneehigh grass
And I often went home with a scraped
knee

Or a dress torn or a finger cut
Down the hill were half built houses
(a place forbidden for me to play)
and scaffolding and bricks scattered
across the path, into the fields.

Sports Day

It is sports day
Ready for the start of my race
Starter raises his pistol
"On your marks"
I crouch down
"Set"
Lean forward
Bang!
I go
I grin
I made a good start
Winning
25 metres
My legs pump like pistons
50 metres
I see Brendon
75 metres
I can not win
too far ahead
dropping back
95 metres
Passed again
I cross the line
Third.

Ian's poem.

A Poem

Once I had an eye operation one November
I went in on a Tuesday, getting used to
the food, people, bed, food.
Hungry all night.
Wednesday morning and needle time, sleepy
I was wheeled away to a white walled room

Needle again, sleepy again.
Sleep.
I awoke on Thursday
Food from Mum and Dad
Lucozade, undrunk
Sour grapes, not tasted
Chocolate?
Home on Thursday

Nick's poem.

5   Now do the same for each of the other two writers.
6   Which poem has changed most?
7   Which poem do you like most?

Now you try

Go through the four stages yourself, following the instructions in the book. See what kind of poem you come up with at the end.

Punctuation

Punctuation makes your writing easier for other people to read. It divides it up into bits a reader can understand.

Sentences

The most important thing is to split your writing up into sentences.

Exercise

1   Look at the picture story. See if you can divide the girl's story up into sentences. Don't worry about punctuation. Just start each sentence on a new line.
2   Study the sentences you have written. Can you explain why you have divided the story up like that?

Three rules for sentences

1   Sentences should begin with a capital letter and end with a full stop.
2   A sentence must make complete sense on its own.

These are proper sentences:

> You're too young to stay out that late!
> Let's go home.

These are not proper sentences:

> Could be one of the best records ever made.
> Mary and me tennis tomorrow.
> Walking along the road after doing the shopping.

3   What you write as a sentence should be one sentence and not several joined together.

This is one sentence:

> Although Jamie reached school in plenty of time, when he got there he realised that he had forgotten his pencil-case, so he hurried home again to fetch it.

This is not one sentence:

> Jamie reached school in plenty of time, at the gate he realised he hadn't got his pencil-case, he hurried home to get it.

It is three sentences:

1   Jamie reached school in plenty of time.
2   At the gate he realised he hadn't got his pencil-case.
3   He hurried home to get it.

Exercise

Each of the following groups of words is a jumbled sentence. Sort the words out to make a complete sentence.

1   surprise got Anna a when home had she
2   large waiting there a her was parcel for
3   what could she wondered be it
4   that her Christmas anything it birthday or wasn't or like
5   disappointed it excitedly was she open very tore but
6   old contained had at Granny's it clothes left her she some house

Exercise

Use each of the following groups of words to make up **one** sentence.

Example: car   level crossing   terrified
Answer :   I was terrified when our car broke down on a level crossing.

1   rhubarb   teacher   shouted
2   soon   Christmas   sorry
3   athlete   angry   stopped
4   holiday   excited   fell
5   mountain   aeroplane   explained

Commas

We use commas to divide a sentence up so that it is easier to read. If you don't use commas in a long sentence, your reader may get lost:

My favourite drinks are Coca-Cola coffee tea lemonade and lime and hot milk.
When we had finished eating David wanted to go and play football.
  Yesterday I met Jan my sister's friend outside the supermarket.

Each of these sentences would be better if it was divided up by commas.

1 Commas are used to separate the different things in a list:

   My favourite drinks are Coca-Cola, coffee, tea, lemonade and lime, and hot milk.

2 They are used to mark off different parts of a sentence, so that it makes sense:

   When we had finished eating, David wanted to go and play football.
   Yesterday I met Jan, my sister's friend, outside the supermarket.

Exercise A

Copy out each of these sentences and put in commas where they are needed:

1 Although my sister's pet rabbit Herman is very tame he sometimes escapes from his hutch.
2 Among the commonest pets in this country are cats dogs hamsters goldfish gerbils and rabbits.
3 Peter will you stop doing that please?
4 When the clock had finished striking my parents went out.
5 Unless I have misunderstood you want a new bike for Christmas.

Exercise B

Copy out these two paragraphs, putting in full stops, capital letters and commas, where they are needed:

i landed with a thump the breath going out of my chest and lay still my face stuck into wet soft earth everything was black around there wasn't a sound the darkness in this hole was thicker than ever and the smell was even grottier

my hand struck wood – planks standing up i ran my finger along it that was funny it was a table a trestle table like dad had in our basement to do his do-it-yourself on i felt better right away a table can't do you any harm there might be chairs as well – I thought – and a sideboard and cupboards and a cooker my hands slid along the top and knocked on something there was a tinny sound my fingers touched metal small and round – a mug and a basin next to it my fingers slipped inside the basin and jerked back of their own accord the inside was all soft and mushy like cloth or leather gone rotten it was weird

Apostrophes

Many people find apostrophes difficult to use properly. There are **two** uses for them. One is easy and the other is more difficult.

1 Apostrophes show where letters have been missed out:

we are → we're
are not → aren't
he is   → he's
I would → I'd

2 Apostrophes also show that something belongs to somebody:

Whose bike is that? It is Mary's bike.
a) If the word ends in -s, just add an apostrophe:
   In our class the girls' exam marks are always better than the boys' results.
b) If the word does not end in -s, then add 's:
   I've got a brother and a sister: my sister's bedroom is always tidier than my brother's.

Special rules

1 **it is** becomes **it's**
   of it is written **its**
2 **who's** means **who is**
   of whom becomes **whose**
3 **yours**   not   **your's**
   hers   not   **her's**
   theirs not   **their's**
   ours   not   **our's**

Exercise C

Write the short form of each of these, using apostrophes where needed:

1   might not
2   should not
3   we were not
4   they are
5   she should have
6   I am not
7   you have not
8   we shall not
9   they will not have done
10 it is not

Exercise D

Read the sentences. Each one contains one or more blanks. Choose the correct word to fill each gap from the words in brackets.

1   I think that's _____ (Peter's/Peters'/Peters) book not _____ (yours'/yours/your's).
2   My _____ (parents/parent's/parents') won't let me go to the new disco.
3   My _____ (parents/parent's/parents') favourite evening out is a trip to the Green Man.
4   I don't know _____ (whos/whose/who's) book this is.
5   I'd like to know _____ (whos/whose/who's) done this.
6   Our football team won _____ (its/it's) first game today.
7   _____ (Its/It's) always interesting to meet your _____ (friends/friend's/friends') friends.
8   Dave and Anne say _____ (their/they're/there) going to the pictures tomorrow.
9   That's our book, not _____ (yours/your's).
10 That's what you _____ (should of/shouldv'e/should've) done.

Writing down what people say

A terrible thing happened to me the other day. I'd arranged to
meet Fiona at the end of King Street where they've got all those
boards up. I'd just got there when this man came up to me. You'll
have to move he said. I told him what I thought of him. I said why
should I? It's a free country. I've got every right to stay where I am.
This is a building site and we're expecting a delivery of he said
walking off sand. Don't say I didn't warn you he shouted and I
looked round just in time to see the lorry.

What's wrong?

Look at the pictures and then read the story. What makes the story difficult to follow?

Punctuating speech

When we write anything that contains the words people say, we must separate out:
the actual words spoken
everything else.

We can do this in one of two ways:
script
direct speech.

Script

Script is how speech is written in plays:

MAN   : Why should I? It's a free country . . . I've got every right to stay where I am.
FOREMAN: This is a building site and we've just had a delivery of . . . (He moves away from him) . . . sand.

1 The names of the characters are written in CAPITAL letters. They come at the beginning of a new line.
2 Put a colon (:) after the name of the speaker.
3 Start the words the character says at the same point on each line.
4 Put explanations and descriptions of what happens in brackets and underline them.

Direct speech

Direct speech is how speech is written in stories:

    I said, 'Why should I? It's a free country . . . I've got every right to stay, where I am.'
    'This is a building site and we're expecting a delivery of . . .,' he said, moving away, '. . . sand.'

1 The words spoken are put in inverted commas:
    '_____' or "_____"
2 Before the first inverted commas you must have either a **comma** (,) or a **colon** (:).
    He said, '_____'
    He said: '_____'
3 When the speech ends you must have one of these:
    , . ? or !
    They come **before** the inverted commas:

    He said, '_____.'
    He said, '_____?'
    He said, '_____!'
    You only use a comma if the sentence is going on:

    '_____,' he said.
4 Each new piece of speech begins with a **capital letter.**
5 When a new person begins speaking, start a new line and go in a bit – this is called **indenting.**
6 When the **he said** words come in the middle of the speech, you don't have to use a capital letter when the speech starts again.

Finish it off

Now write the whole conversation:
a) in script
b) in direct speech.

Working with words

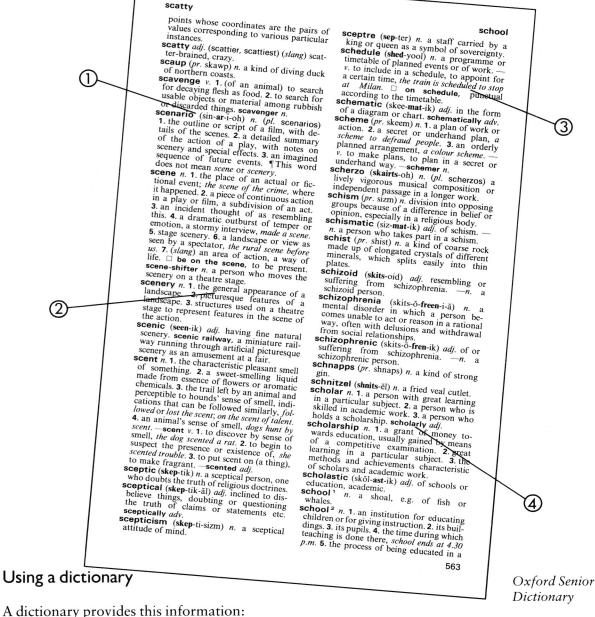

Oxford Senior
Dictionary

Using a dictionary

A dictionary provides this information:

1 It tells you how words should be pronounced.

2 It tells you the meaning(s) of the word.

3 It gives examples of how the word is used.

4 It shows how the word can be built up into new words.

Exercise A

Use the dictionary page to work out how to say each of these words:

scherzo   scenario   sceptic
schism   schnapps   scaup

Exercise B

Use a dictionary to work out how to pronounce these words:

igneous   palliasse   chamois
breviary   oleander   xenolith

Exercise C

Find out the meaning of each of the following words, and then use it correctly in a sentence you have made up. All the words are on the dictionary page opposite.

schnitzel   schedule   sceptre
schist   scavenge   scholar

Exercise D

In the sentences that follow, each of the gaps can be filled by one of the words on the dictionary page. Work out which word fits each gap.

1   He was mentally disturbed and the doctor said he was suffering from _____.

2   I think he was talking nonsense because he had drunk too much _____.

3   My brother works in the theatre as a _____.

4   In the film we saw a _____ of porpoises swimming alongside the boat.

5   The trouble with this bus service is that the buses are never on _____.

6   _____ is a good rock to climb on, because it gives a good grip.

Exercise E

1   Use a dictionary to find out the meaning of these words:

bonsai   clerihew   ibex
puce   taffeta   xenon

2   For each word write a sentence using it correctly.

Exercise F

Use a dictionary to work out the correct spelling for each of the missing words.

1   I never know _____ (weather/wether/whether) you're telling the truth or not.

2   We wrote to the hotel to find out if there was _____ (accomodation/acommodation/accommodation) available.

3   My bed has got a very lumpy _____. (mattress/matress/matrice)

4   That's a problem which I think we ought to _____. (discus/disscuss/discuss)

5   In the film the only good man was the _____ (sherrif/sheriff/sherriff) of Dodge City.

6   One of the _____ (pedals/peddles/pedels) on my bike is broken.

7   During the match one of the players _____. (colapsed/callapsed/collapsed)

8   I don't _____ (posess/possess/posses) a white shirt.

9   You must _____ (fulfill/fullfill/fulfil) your promise.

10   He hasn't got a _____ (licence/lisence/license) for his dog.

Word building

Words can be extended, like houses:

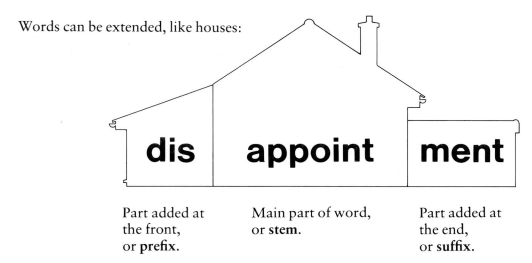

Part added at
the front,
or **prefix**.

Main part of word,
or **stem**.

Part added at
the end,
or **suffix**.

In this way one simple stem can be built up
into several longer words:

prefix	stem	suffix
un		d
dis	place	s
re		ment

Exercise

1 Write down all the words you can make
   from this word-building diagram.
2 Use three of the words in separate
   sentences of your own.
3 Now make similar word-building
   diagrams for each of these words:
      weight
      fool
      stop
      manage
      measure

Another way in which words can be built up
is by combining them with other words:

    play + back
           bill
           boy
           ground
           mate
           pen
           school
           thing
           time
           wright

Exercise

1 Make sure that you know what each of
   these words means.
2 Choose three of them and use them in
   separate sentences of your own.
3 Make similar word-combination lists for
   each of these words:
      run
      head
      school
      foot

Prefixes

Prefixes usually change or add to the meaning of the stem.

Group A
dis-   in-   non-

Group B
anti-   pro-
pre-   post-
maxi-   mini-
stereo-   mono-

Group C
multi-
centi-
milli-
kilo-
semi-

Exercise

1   Each of the prefixes in Group A means **not**. Find words containing each of them, illustrating this meaning.

2   The words in Group B are in pairs.
   a) Find words beginning with each prefix.
   b) Explain what each prefix means.
   c) Explain why they are paired in this way.

3   The prefixes in Group C all have something in common.
   a) Find words beginning with each prefix.
   b) Explain what each prefix means.
   c) Explain what they all have in common.

Suffixes

Suffixes alter the way in which a stem can be used in a sentence.

Example
hope : I **hope** that you will help.
hopeful : I am very **hopeful**.
hopefully : It is better to travel **hopefully**.

A   -able   -ible   -ble
B   -ly
C   -er   -est
D   -ful
E   -tion   -ion   -sion
F   -ise   -ize
G   -less

Exercise

1   For each group of suffixes find an example of a word that ends in this way.
2   Use each word in a sentence of your own.
3   See if you can explain how each suffix changes the way in which the stem can be used.

For the teacher

The focus in this book is on presenting a wide range of practical and progressive language activities in as accessible and entertaining a way as possible. The main part of the book is arranged thematically so that topics likely to engage children's interest and imagination are readily available. It also offers a systematic introduction to important language techniques such as narrative, exposition, and the expression of opinion.

Themes

There are six theme units; they contain the following elements:

Starter A visual and practical introduction to the theme.

Activities Reading, writing, listening, and talking deriving from some aspect of the theme. Activities pages open up the theme and also give opportunities for practising particular techniques.

Techniques Each theme unit contains at least one spread which focuses on a specific language technique:

Puzzles Reading activities such as cloze and sequencing exercises, word games and other puzzles.

Reading A longer and more demanding passage, usually prose fiction, but occasionally verse. While we have tried to ensure that all other texts and instructions are at a level that average readers can cope with reasonably easily, the reading pages are deliberately more challenging. Many teachers will wish to introduce this material by reading it to the class. The stories and extracts have been chosen for their variety, imaginative interest, and humour.

Using theme units We envisage that each two-page spread should normally provide material for two timetable periods. Some will take longer to complete. All activities are clearly signalled and written work is usually preceded by preparatory activities.

Once the 'Starter' has been used, the teacher has a choice of route through the unit. This can be summed up in this diagram:

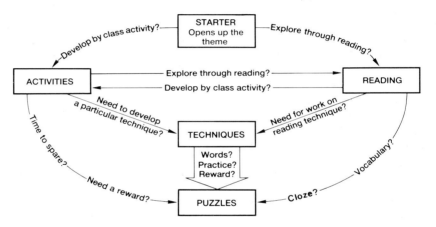

Specials

These are 2-page or 4-page units designed to be used in a different way. There is a strong element of play in them. Most of them present a story or situation usually by means of some kind of evidence — pictures, documents etc. The children have to find their way through this by playing a game, working out a story, or in some other way that challenges their intelligence and imagination. Specials are usually suitable for use either individually or in pairs or small groups. While we hope that children will enjoy them, there is a serious language-teaching purpose behind each of them.

Reference section

The 'nuts and bolts' of writing are presented in reference form with exercises. These are separate from the rest of the book for ease of use, either individually or in class.

Acknowledgements

The publishers would like to thank the following for permission to reproduce photographs and other copyright material:

The Architectural Press p. 20 (centre left and bottom right); **Barnaby's Picture Library** p. 69 (top); **Bristol Journal** p. 45; **Bus and Coach Council** p. 85; **J. Allan Cash** p. 20 (centre right and bottom right); **Compix** p. 12; **Country Living/Dolores Fairman** p. 75 (top left); **Edifice** p. 20 (top left); **Ford** p. 85; **BBC Hulton Picture Library** pp. 78, 85; **IPC Magazines** pp. 60, 61; **Rob Judges** pp. 20 (top right), 26 (both), 31 (all), 63 (both), 76 (all), 108–109 (all), 110–111 (all); **MIZZ Magazine** p. 75 (bottom left and centre); **Mountain Camera/John Cleare** p. 69 (bottom); **John Seely** pp. 46, 47; **SKY Magazine** p. 75 (bottom right); **SONY** p. 85; **Syndication International** pp. 69 (top), 75 (top right); **Topham Picture Library** p. 79.

The illustrations are by: David Ace, Martin Aitchison, Hemesh Alles, Derek Brazell, Andrew Brown, Judy Brown, Helen Charlton, Helen Clipson, Peter Elson, Robina Green, Chris Hill, Sue Heap, David Jackson, Christyan Jones, Peter Joyce, Kim Lane, Maggie Ling, Alan Marks, Ian Miller, Chris Molan, Tony Morris, Oxford Illustrators, Helen Parsley, Joanna Quinn, R D H Artists, Shoo Rayner, Hilary Saville, Susan Scott, Nick Sharratt, Kate Taylor, Brian Walker, Joanna Williams, Shaun Williams and Galina Zolfaghari. Cover illustration by Christina Brimage.

The publishers would like to thank the following for permission to reprint copyright material.

Joan Aiken: extract from *The Shadow Guests* (Cape, 1980). Reprinted by permission of A.M. Heath & Co. Ltd. **Bernard Ashley:** 'Equal Rights' from *Openings* ed. R. Blatchford (Bell & Hymans Ltd). **P.S. Blackman Jr.:** 'I Thought a Lot of You' from *City Lines*. Reprinted by permission of ILEA English Centre. **John Branfield:** extract from *A Fox in Winter* (Gollancz, 1980). Reprinted by permission of Victor Gollancz Ltd. *The Bristol Journal:* 'Here's to you, lovely little Lisa!' from *The Bristol Journal*, 20.2.86. Used with permission. **Betsy Byars:** extract from *The TV Kid*. Reprinted by permission of The Bodley Head on behalf of Betsy Byars. **Italo Calvino:** extract from *Italian Folktales*, translated by George Martin (Penguin 1982), copyright © Giulio Einaudi Editore, s.p.a., as *Fiabe Italiane* 1956, translation copyright © Harcourt Brace Jovanovich Inc., 1980. Reprinted by permission of Penguin Books Ltd. **Roald Dahl:** 'The Caravan' and 'My Father' from *Danny Champion of the World*. Reprinted by permission of Jonathan Cape Ltd., for the author. **Anne Frank:** Reprinted from Anne Frank's *Diary* by permission of Vallentine, Mitchell & Co., Ltd. **C.A. Lejeune:** extract from *Thank You For Having Me*. Reprinted by permission of Anthony Lejeune. **Robert Leeson:** extracts from *Challenge in the Dark* (Collins, 1978). Reprinted by permission of Collins Publishers. **David Line:** extract from *Run For Your Life*. Reprinted by permission of Jonathan Cape Ltd., for the author. **Edwin Muir:** extract from *Autobiography*. Reprinted by permission of The Hogarth Press on behalf of Gavin Muir. **Brian Patten:** 'Billy Dreamer's Fantastic Friends' from *Gargling With Jelly* (Kestrel Books, 1985), copyright © Brian Patten, 1985, pp. 24–5. Reprinted by permission of Penguin Books Ltd. **J.B. Phillips:** extract from *Gospels in Modern English* (Fontana, 1957). Reprinted by permission of Collins Publishers. **Michael Rosen:** 'I'm the youngest in our house' from *Wouldn't You Like to Know* (André Deutsch, 1977). Reprinted by permission of the publisher. **Vernon Scannell:** 'Camping Out' from *A Puffin Quintet of Poets*. Reprinted by permission of the author. **Maureen Stewart:** extract from *Dear Emily* (Penguin, 1986). Reprinted by permission of Penguin Books Australia Ltd. **John Walsh:** 'Blind Boy on the Shore' from *A Puffin Quintet of Poets*. Reprinted by permission of Mrs A.M. Walsh. **Kit Wright:** 'Dave Dirt Came to Dinner' from *Hot Dog and Other Poems* (Kestrel Books, 1981), copyright © Kit Wright, 1981, p. 61. Reprinted by permission of Penguin Books Ltd.

Although every effort has been made to contact copyright holders this has not been possible in a few instances. We apologise for any apparent negligence.